JUICING FOR B. ....ERS

The ultimate guide to a leaner, more energetic soul -
1500 days to lose weight, fight aging and recharge
energy with quick and tasty centrifuge recipes

ROSA HURLBUTT

Table of Content

Introduction

From the earliest moments of mankind's understanding of the world, we've sought to harness its marvels and transform them into tangible experiences. Among the wonders of nature, the tantalizing allure of fruits and vegetables stands unmatched, each holding a unique story, an essence waiting to be unraveled. Delve deep, and you'll find an alchemical instrument capable of turning these natural treasures into elixirs of life, an apparatus that embodies the harmony of science and art: the centrifuge. Let's embark on a journey where engineering meets enchantment, and where every spin is a serenade to nature.

Welcome to Your Juicing Journey

The heart of every adventure lies in taking that first step, and if you're reading this, congratulations. You've already set foot on a transformative path, one that promises not only tantalizing flavors but a symphony of health benefits: your very own juicing journey. Like any meaningful pursuit, it is neither the destination nor the start, but the experiences along the way that truly count. As you traverse this path, you'll discover the art, the science, and the sheer joy of merging nature's gifts into luscious sips of goodness.

Imagine standing at the threshold of a vast orchard. Every tree and plant pulsates with life, and you can almost hear the whisper of stories each one has to tell. In your hands lies the potential to unlock those tales, weaving them into a narrative that's uniquely yours. This is the promise of juicing. It isn't just about extracting liquid from fruits and vegetables; it's about unlocking nature's memoirs, one glass at a time.

Let's take a brief stroll down memory lane. There was a time when the act of savoring a juicy orange or a crisp apple was an event in itself. Every bite was a direct dialogue with the land, a tale of sunshine, rain, and the tender care of farmers. Today, while we may live in an age of fast foods and instant gratifications, the craving for that genuine connection with our food has never quite disappeared. It has simply evolved. And juicing, in its most authentic essence, bridges that temporal gap, reacquainting us with the roots of our sustenance.

At this juncture, you might ask, why juice? Why not just consume fruits and vegetables in their whole form? Valid question. And while there's undeniable value in savoring these natural wonders in their original state, juicing introduces an element of alchemy. By merging different ingredients, you're not just creating a beverage; you're crafting an elixir. A potion that can be tailored to your mood, your nutritional needs, or even the call of a particular season. Autumn might beckon a hearty blend of beets and pomegranates, while a summer's day might inspire a refreshing concoction of watermelon and mint. The possibilities are as endless as they are delightful.

It's essential, however, to remember that this journey isn't merely about the end product. It's about the process. The act of choosing your ingredients, understanding their origins, appreciating their textures, and eventually watching them transform is therapeutic. It's meditation in motion. Every fruit you peel, every vegetable you chop, and every herb you tear is a tactile reminder of the world's richness. And as your juicer hums to life, extracting vibrant hues and aromas, you become an integral part of that tapestry, a weaver of stories and flavors.

As you embark on this odyssey, you'll undoubtedly encounter a myriad of experiences. There will be days of exuberance, where every blend you create feels like a masterpiece, an ode to nature's bounty. Then there might be moments of introspection, perhaps even frustration, when a particular mix doesn't quite meet your expectations. And that's alright. Because every drop, every taste, and every aroma is a lesson, a stepping stone on your ever-evolving path.

There's also a certain romance to juicing, one that's often overlooked. It's in the way sunlight filters through a glass of ruby-red beet juice, casting dancing shadows. Or how the aroma of freshly juiced pineapples can instantly transport you to a sun-kissed tropical paradise, even if just for a fleeting moment. It's in these nuances, these silent dialogues with nature, that the true essence of juicing shines.

As you continue to explore, you'll also find that juicing isn't a solitary endeavor. It's a communion. Sharing a freshly crafted juice with a loved one, watching their eyes light up with surprise or delight, is an experience in itself. It's an unspoken bond, a silent toast to health, happiness, and the countless wonders that nature bestows upon us.

The Power of the Centrifuge: Unveiling the Magic

As a child, did you ever gaze in awe at a magician pulling a rabbit out of a hat? Or perhaps you were enchanted by the illusionist who seemed to effortlessly levitate above the ground? The world of magic is rife with moments that baffle our understanding and ignite our curiosity. Yet, in our daily lives, there exists a tool that, with its unique alchemy, rivals the allure of the most skilled magician: the centrifuge. And while its magic might not involve white doves or disappearing acts, the power it wields in the realm of juicing is nothing short of spectacular.

The centrifuge. A name that might initially evoke images of complex laboratories or intricate machinery. Yet, at its core, this contraption operates on a beautifully simple principle: the power of rapid rotation to separate substances of different densities. It's like an elegant dance, where the centrifuge pirouettes at dizzying speeds, gracefully separating the dense pulp from the luscious juice, allowing us to experience the pure, unadulterated essence of nature's offerings.

Let's set the stage with a visualization. Picture an apple, ripe and radiant in its crimson glory. As it stands, this apple is a delightful mix of fibrous content, juicy segments, seeds, and skin. Now, introduce this apple to the centrifuge. Within moments, what emerges is a liquid that captures the soul of that apple – its aroma, its flavor, and its vitality. It's akin to extracting the very essence of a symphony, isolating the soul-stirring solo that makes the heart race.

But how does this mechanical marvel achieve such a feat? While it's tempting to leave it shrouded in mystery, understanding its workings only deepens our appreciation. At its heart, the centrifuge uses the force generated by its rapid spin. As it whirls into action, the heavier components—like the pulp and seeds—are flung outward, while the lighter, liquid essence is carefully channeled into a waiting receptacle. It's as if the centrifuge, with its balletic grace, is the ultimate maestro, orchestrating a performance where each component knows its place.

Consider, for instance, the complexity of a fruit like the pineapple. Encased in its spiky armor is a treasure trove of golden nectar. But amidst that sweetness are tough fibers, a core that's rigid, and an outer skin that's anything but palatable. It's a fortress, seemingly impervious. Yet, within the centrifuge's chamber, this fortress yields, revealing its hidden ambrosia. And in that moment, the centrifuge isn't just a machine; it's an artisan, skillfully extracting the elixir while leaving behind the undesired.

Now, while the centrifuge's prowess in separating is unparalleled, it's essential to recognize that it does more than just that. It elevates the experience. The juices that emerge from its embrace are vibrant, both in color and flavor. They're a concentrated burst of nature, where every sip is like a sonnet, an ode to the fruit or vegetable it originated from.

Yet, for all its technical brilliance, the centrifuge's charm lies in its accessibility. It doesn't demand of you an understanding of its intricate physics or a mastery of complex techniques. Instead, it invites you with open arms, asking only for your curiosity and your passion for exploration. Whether you're a seasoned chef, a health enthusiast, or someone taking their first steps into the world of juicing, the centrifuge ensures that the magic remains within reach.

And speaking of magic, let's dwell on a slightly poetic notion. The centrifuge doesn't just separate; it tells stories. Every drop of juice it extracts carries with it tales of sun-soaked orchards, of gentle breezes, of the dedicated hands that nurtured the produce. So, when you take that first sip of juice, freshly crafted from the centrifuge, you're not merely tasting a beverage. You're partaking in a narrative, one that speaks of the earth, the skies, and everything in between.

Our voyage into the mesmerizing world of the centrifuge reaffirms that the boundaries between art and science are but mere illusions. With every rotation, this magnificent tool weaves the tales of nature into a liquid symphony, allowing us to experience the world in its purest form. As we take a moment to appreciate the radiant elixirs before us, we're reminded that magic isn't just found in fairytales or grand illusions—it's right there in our kitchens, in the dance of the centrifuge, in every drop that captures the soul of the earth. So, as we raise our glasses to the beauty of juicing, let's also toast to the innovations that make these moments possible.

Part I: The Foundation of Juicing

Chapter 1: The Whys and Hows of Juicing

Juicing is more than a simple extraction of liquids from fruits and vegetables; it's an alchemy of flavors, health, and understanding. Behind the emerald green kale juice or the fiery red beet concoction lies a myriad of complexities, both in process and purpose. Every droplet tells a tale— of nature's bounty, the wisdom of extraction, and the pursuit of health. And while the vibrant allure of freshly squeezed juices beckons, knowing the underlying mechanisms and the art of drawing out optimal nutrition elevates the experience from mere consumption to a conscious act of nourishment.

Understanding the Mechanism of Juicing

When we think of alchemy, our minds might wander to ancient labs filled with mysterious concoctions and fabled transmutations, but isn't our very kitchen a modern sanctum of culinary alchemy? At the heart of this realm lies an art both ageless and revolutionary: juicing. The act of transforming solid into liquid, of capturing essence and flavor in its most elemental form. But what precisely happens during this metamorphosis? Let's traverse this delectable landscape and unravel the science behind the mechanism of juicing.

Juicing is not merely a process; it's a poetic dance between physics and nature. The journey begins with the meticulous selection of the freshest fruits and vegetables, each possessing its own unique profile of water content, fiber structure, and nutrients. The chosen produce then steps onto the grand stage of our juicer, awaiting the spectacular transformation.

Now, imagine peering into an opera house from a balcony. From that vantage point, we see the orchestra pit, the actors, and the props, all playing their respective roles. In our kitchen opera, the juicer assumes the role of the maestro, guiding each component to its crescendo. The blades, the sieve, and the spout become the instruments through which our produce's symphony is orchestrated.

But how do these elements come together to perform this magical extraction? It begins with the force. Not in a galaxy far, far away, but right in our juicer. The initial contact between the fruit or vegetable and the blade generates a force. This force, in turn, disrupts the cell walls of the produce. Picture an ancient fortress with walls designed to protect its treasures. The produce's cell walls are analogous to these fortresses, safeguarding the precious juices within. The blades' forceful dance causes these walls to crumble, releasing the juices that have been held captive.

Yet, not all juices are the same. The consistency and quality of the liquid extracted can vary based on the nature of the produce. For instance, consider the deep, lush liquidity of watermelon versus the thick, velvety texture of an avocado. The juicer's architecture understands these nuances. Its design ensures that each produce, regardless of its intrinsic qualities, is handled with care, optimizing the extraction process.

However, the mechanism doesn't stop at mere extraction. There's a sophisticated filtration system at play. As the blades whirl and twirl, the liquid essence finds its way through a meticulously designed sieve. This sieve, a mesh-like structure, ensures that only the finest juice reaches our glass, leaving behind the pulp and any unwanted residues. It's a ballet of precision, where every drop is choreographed to perfection, ensuring we get the purest of nectars.

While the juice is the hero of this narrative, the pulp, often overlooked, plays a crucial role too. This fibrous residue acts as a testament to the efficiency of the juicing process. A drier pulp indicates a more effective extraction, a sign that our juicer has performed its role with aplomb. On the other hand, if the pulp feels wet and retains significant moisture, it might be time to reconsider the efficiency of our juicing method.

But perhaps the most mesmerizing aspect of this entire mechanism is its universality. Whether one is in a bustling New York kitchen or amidst the serenity of a Tuscan countryside home, the principles remain constant. The centrifugal force, the sieve's meticulous filtration, and the dance of extraction are universal truths in the realm of juicing.

Beyond the technicalities, there's an underlying emotion to this mechanism. When we juice, we're not just extracting liquid; we're distilling memories, emotions, and experiences. The orange juice that reminds us of sun-kissed mornings, the green juice that takes us back to health resolutions, or the beetroot blend that brings forth nostalgia of garden harvests. Each glass holds a story, a narrative crafted by the intricate mechanism that transforms solid to liquid.

To truly appreciate the beauty of juicing, one must understand its mechanism, its rhythm, and its soul. For in every drop of juice, there's a universe of science and sentiment, waiting to be sipped, savored, and celebrated.

Extracting Maximum Nutritional Value

Juicing, with its verdant allure and siren song of wellness, beckons to both novice and aficionado alike. Beyond the vibrant hues and intoxicating aromas, lies a more profound mission: the quest for nutritional gold. But how do we ensure that each droplet of juice we extract is not just a cocktail of flavors, but a potent elixir brimming with the best of nature's offerings?

Think of juicing as an art form—a canvas where produce is the paint, and the juicer, our brush. But, akin to art, the quality of the final masterpiece isn't merely dictated by the tools and mediums employed; it's about technique, understanding, and a touch of magic.

Let's embark on a journey—a quest, if you will—to harness the full nutritional spectrum of our chosen ingredients.

Every fruit, every vegetable, has its own intricate map of nutrients. Vitamins, minerals, antioxidants, and enzymes form a complex network within. And while it's tempting to believe that crushing or grinding these would automatically release their benefits into our juice, reality is slightly more nuanced.

Heat and oxidation are two notorious villains in our story. The friction caused by some juicers can introduce heat, which in turn can diminish the potency of certain nutrients. Oxidation, the interaction of juice with air, is another arch-nemesis, causing degradation of vitamins and other vital compounds.

The key then is to minimize the time our produce spends being processed and its exposure to air. Here's where the design and function of our juicer come into play. Masticating juicers, with their slow and deliberate extraction, often take the lead in preserving nutritional integrity, as they generate less heat. Centrifugal juicers, while efficient, can sometimes be a tad more aggressive, causing a bit more heat and oxidation. But fear not, with proper technique and care, even they can produce nutritionally-rich juices.

Water-soluble vitamins, like Vitamin C, are the fragile poets of the nutrient world. They're delicate, sensitive to heat, light, and air. To maximize their presence in our juice, it's crucial to consume the elixir as soon as it's made or to store it in airtight, opaque containers if needed for later.

Then there are phytonutrients—nature's arsenal of disease-fighting, health-promoting compounds. These often give fruits and vegetables their vibrant colors. Lycopene in tomatoes, anthocyanins in berries, and beta-carotene in carrots are just a few. The good news? They're relatively stable but do prefer a cool environment. So, if you're juicing to store, the refrigerator becomes your elixir's best friend.

Enzymes, the catalysts of the food world, play pivotal roles in digestion and nutrient absorption. They're heat-sensitive sprites, which means the cooler the juicing process, the better. This makes cold-pressed or masticating juicers a darling among those keen on preserving enzymatic activity.

It's also worth noting that not all fruits and veggies should be treated equally in the juicing realm. Citrus fruits, with their zest brimming with essential oils and potent phytonutrients, require a gentle hand. Instead of thrusting them wholly into a juicer, consider peeling (while retaining as much of the white pith as possible) to ensure a harmonious blend of tart, sweet, and nutritious.

Leafy greens, with their intricate cellular structures, ask for a slow, deliberate press. Their nutritional treasures—chlorophyll, vitamins, and minerals—demand patience and care. A hurried extraction might leave a significant chunk of their goodness behind.

But perhaps the most profound of considerations is the produce's origin. Fresh, organically grown fruits and vegetables, free from pesticides and bursting with nature's essence, are your ticket to a nutritionally opulent juice. Their conventionally grown counterparts might look similar but often lag in the nutrient department due to soil depletion and chemical exposure.

In this enthralling endeavor, it's not just about the act of juicing. It's about the choices we make, the understanding we wield, and the techniques we employ. It's a dance—a delicate ballet of balance, care, and knowledge. Each fruit, each vegetable has its rhythm, its pulse, and to extract its maximum nutritional value is to honor its essence, its very life force.

In this glass, holding the luminous liquid, you're not just holding juice. You're holding a potion— a concoction of nature's best, amplified by knowledge and crafted with love. It's not just about quenching thirst; it's about nourishing the soul. Drink deep, and let the magic unfold.

Chapter 2: The Vital Ingredients - Fruits and Vegetables Demystified

Nature, in its infinite wisdom, has painted a vibrant spectrum of fruits and vegetables for us to savor and nourish our bodies. Each hue signifies a symphony of flavors, textures, and vital nutrients, uniquely crafted by the environment's melody and time's rhythm. This chapter delves deep into this colorful realm, unraveling the mysteries behind each shade and understanding the dance of seasonality that dictates when and how nature's bounties reach their prime.

Color Palette: Unlocking Nutrients and Benefits

Nature, in its boundless generosity, offers us a mesmerizing array of fruits and vegetables, each distinct not only in taste but also in hue. This vibrant spectrum is not just a visual feast but an indicator of the unique nutrients and benefits nestled within each offering. Delving into this colorful realm is akin to exploring a painter's palette, where each shade tells its own tale of wellness and vitality.

When we observe the brilliant crimson of a ripe tomato or the deep purple of a juicy plum, we aren't merely witnessing a color. We're beholding a hint, a whisper of the nutritional symphony it brings forth. It's nature's way of packaging health benefits with visual cues, a secret code waiting to be deciphered by those willing to listen.

The vermilion and scarlet hues that peppers, tomatoes, and strawberries don are primarily due to the presence of lycopene, a powerful antioxidant. It's an artistic brushstroke that hints at potential benefits for heart health and cancer risk reduction. This is not just a pigment, but a shield, guarding our cells against the relentless assault of free radicals.

Emerald green, the shade of lush forests and verdant meadows, graces our plates in the form of spinach, kale, and broccoli. This hue sings the song of chlorophyll, which not only gives plants their green brilliance but also carries potential detoxifying properties for our bodies. Delve deeper, and one discovers that these greens are also treasure troves of folate, iron, and calcium, each nutrient weaving its own narrative of health and vitality.

Our journey across the palette takes us next to the sunlit yellows and oranges of bell peppers, carrots, and citrus fruits. These sunny shades are the canvas of carotenoids, particularly beta-carotene, which the body masterfully converts into vitamin A. It's more than a pigment; it's a promise of improved vision, immune function, and skin health. Here, in these bright bites, is nature's own sunlight, captured and condensed for our nourishment.

Venturing into the deep purples and blues, we encounter the magic of anthocyanins found in blueberries, eggplants, and blackberries. These colors, reminiscent of twilight skies and deep oceans, harbor potential protective properties against oxidative stress. Moreover, this dusky spectrum may hold keys to cognitive health and memory enhancement. Each bite is like diving into a midnight sea, rich in mysteries and potent benefits.

Then there are the whites and beiges, often overlooked in the clamor for more vivid colors but equally essential. Think of mushrooms, garlic, and onions. These may not parade in the flamboyant hues of their counterparts, but they carry allicin and other compounds with potential benefits ranging from heart health to antimicrobial properties. In their subdued shades lies a quiet strength, a muted yet profound assertion of their worth.

It's essential to realize that this color-coded system of nature isn't just about individual benefits. The true magic unfolds when we combine these shades on our plate, creating a mosaic of health benefits. Each hue complements the other, leading to a harmonious balance. For instance, the vitamin C in a bright orange bell pepper can enhance the absorption of iron from the dark green spinach. It's a dance of nutrients, a choreography of wellness where each color plays its unique part but together creates a masterpiece of health.

In essence, the vast palette of fruits and vegetables isn't just a culinary delight but a roadmap to health. Each color, each hue, is a chapter in the grand narrative of wellness, waiting to be embraced and celebrated. By understanding this chromatic language of nature, we unlock the doors to a realm where every bite is a brushstroke, painting our health in the most vibrant shades imaginable. The next time you gaze at a rainbow of fruits and vegetables, remember you're not just looking at colors; you're gazing upon stories, each narrating tales of wellness, vitality, and life.

Seasonality and Selecting the Best Produce

When nature crafts its produce, it follows an intricate rhythm—a rhythm dictated by the turn of the Earth, the dance of the seasons, and the song of time. Every fruit, every vegetable, has its own moment of glory, a brief window when it stands at the pinnacle of taste and nutrition. To harness the true potential of what nature offers, one must not just understand but truly resonate with the symphony of seasonality.

Imagine a sun-drenched summer day. The warmth is palpable, and the air is thick with the hum of life. This season of golden sunlight and azure skies beckons a particular set of produce to take center stage. Juicy watermelons, succulent peaches, and crisp cucumbers are but a few of summer's star performers. Their taste is the taste of summer itself—vivid, intense, and bursting with life. But what makes these summer delights so special?

It's the alignment of nature's factors. The extended daylight, the heightened temperatures, and the specific soil conditions converge to create the perfect milieu for these fruits and vegetables to flourish. When consumed in their prime season, they don't just offer superior taste but also a richer nutrient profile. It's nature's way of saying, "Now is the moment."

As summer gives way to the mellow mellowness of autumn, the cast of produce on nature's grand stage shifts. Now, it's the turn of apples, with their crisp bite and sweet-tart flavor, or pumpkins, with their earthy sweetness, to shine. Their flavors evoke images of golden leaves and cozy evenings, but they also bring forth a treasure of nutrients tailored for the season. Nature, in its wisdom, knows that as the weather turns cooler, our bodies need different sustenance. And so, it provides.

Winter, with its stark landscapes and chilled breezes, has its own set of heroes. Root vegetables like turnips and beets delve deep into the earth, drawing nutrients and emerging as powerhouses of sustenance to help us navigate the cold. Citrus fruits, vibrant and zesty, offer a burst of vitamin C, armoring us against winter ailments.

When spring pirouettes into the scene, it brings a tender freshness, a promise of new beginnings. This season of blooms and gentle warmth graces us with greens like spinach and arugula and fruits like strawberries. Their flavors are delicate, mirroring the softness of spring, but their nutrient content is anything but. They provide the necessary vitality to shake off winter's inertia and embrace the burgeoning life around.

While understanding seasonality offers a guide to when produce is at its prime, selecting the best specimens requires an additional layer of knowledge. One must be attuned to the subtle signs that nature provides. For instance, a ripe tomato has a deep, even color and yields slightly under gentle pressure, while a fresh cucumber is firm to the touch with a vibrant skin.

Furthermore, while appearances can be a good indicator, they shouldn't be the sole determinant. A perfectly shaped apple might look appealing, but sometimes, the slightly imperfect ones, with a little blemish here or a tiny spot there, might be the most flavorful. It's a reminder that nature, in its authenticity, doesn't always conform to our notions of perfection. Instead, it revels in genuine expression, and often, it's in this genuineness that the truest flavors and nutrients reside.

Another factor to consider is the origin. Local produce, grown close to where it's consumed, often has an edge in terms of freshness. It hasn't traveled long distances, and hence, hasn't been subjected to extended periods of storage or preservatives to prolong its shelf life. The shorter the journey from farm to plate, the likelier it is that the produce retains its optimal flavor and nutritional value.

In the grand theater of life, seasonality is the script that nature writes and revises year after year, with unfaltering precision. Embracing this seasonal ebb and flow allows us to dine not just with our taste buds but with our very souls. It's a communion, a moment of profound connection with the world around us. And in this connection lies the secret to extracting the truest essence, the deepest flavors, and the most potent nutrients from our fruits and vegetables. Every season, every fruit, every vegetable has a story. Our role? To listen, to understand, and to savor.

Chapter 3: Equip Yourself: A Comprehensive Guide to Juicers

In our pursuit of health and wellness, the tools we equip ourselves with often play as crucial a role as the choices we make. Among these tools, the juicer has emerged as an emblem of our commitment to nourishing our bodies with the purest of essences. Yet, as with any cherished instrument, understanding its intricacies and ensuring its upkeep are paramount to deriving the best value. Journey with us as we delve deep into the world of juicers, demystifying their types, and shedding light on the rituals of care that keep them at their prime.

Types of Juicers and Their Efficacies

In the alchemical world of juicing, the juicer is our modern-day philosopher's stone. The quest for extracting that golden elixir from fruits and vegetables hinges significantly upon this magical apparatus. While the idea might sound simple enough—turn solid produce into liquid—the orchestra of mechanics and design that goes into every juicer is nothing short of a marvel.

When embarking on the pilgrimage of selecting the perfect juicer, it's not uncommon to feel like a child standing at the entrance of a vast toy store, eyes wide, heart racing with anticipation. The sheer diversity of options, each with its set of promises and peculiarities, can be dizzying.

At the heart of the conundrum lies the question: What are you really looking for in a juicer? The answer, of course, varies from person to person. Some might be in pursuit of sheer power, others in the finesse of extraction, and yet others might prioritize ease and speed.

Centrifugal juicers, for instance, are the speed demons of the juicing world. They use a fast-spinning blade against a mesh filter, transforming produce into juice in a matter of seconds. Their prowess lies in their ability to handle vast quantities quickly. Imagine wanting to whip up a fresh orange juice for an impromptu gathering of friends or to invigorate a Monday morning before heading to work. In such moments, the centrifugal juicer becomes your best companion. Yet, with great speed comes a certain compromise. These machines tend to be louder and might not extract as much juice from leafy greens.

On the other end of the spectrum, we find masticating juicers. These are the contemplative poets of the juicing universe. They operate slowly, chewing and grinding the produce to extract juice. The word 'masticate' literally means to chew, and that's precisely what these juicers do. Their unhurried process ensures a higher yield, especially with tougher greens like kale or spinach. Moreover, the juice tends to be less frothy and lasts longer due to reduced oxidation. The symphony of a masticating juicer, however, isn't for everyone. Their deliberate pace can be a point of contention for those always in a hurry.

Then, there are the triturating juicers, or twin-gear machines. Think of them as the seasoned maestros, conducting an intricate ballet of extraction. They possess two gears that rotate inwards, grinding and pressing the produce between them. Their efficacy lies in their ability to handle a vast array of produce, from the softest berries to the toughest wheatgrass, all while ensuring minimal heat and oxidation. The result? A juice brimming with nutrients and vitality. Such masterful performance, though, comes with a steeper learning curve and price tag.

Beyond these three, the realm of juicers extends into more specialized territories. For instance, the hydraulic press juicers, often revered by hardcore enthusiasts, use tremendous pressure to squeeze juice out of the produce. Their claim to fame is the unparalleled quality and quantity of juice they produce. Yet, their intricate design and heftier cost make them a choice for the truly dedicated.

Citrus juicers, focusing singularly on citrus fruits, offer simplicity in design and function. They are straightforward, often manual, and evoke a sense of nostalgia. Perfect for those lazy Sunday mornings when all you crave is a glass of fresh-squeezed orange or grapefruit juice.

It's crucial to recognize that there's no universal 'best' juicer. The beauty lies in understanding your unique needs, desires, and lifestyle. While one person's treasure might be the centrifugal juicer for its sheer velocity, another might find solace in the rhythmic dance of a masticating machine.

In the end, the essence of juicing transcends beyond the machine. It's about the alchemy of transformation, taking the raw, the whole, and distilling it into its purest liquid form. The juicer you choose becomes an extension of this personal journey, a trusted ally in the quest for nourishment and vitality. So, as you stand at that vast store's entrance, remember that the magic doesn't just lie in the machine, but in the hands and heart of the person using it.

Cleaning, Maintenance, and Tips

In the sacred temple of our kitchens, where culinary wizardry unfolds daily, the juicer stands tall as both an emblem of health and a beacon of delight. Yet, as with all prized possessions, it demands respect not just in its operation but also in its upkeep. The euphoria of that freshly poured, shimmering glass of juice can be short-lived if confronted with the aftermath of pulp-laden parts and sticky residues. How does one ensure that this symbol of nourishment doesn't become a tedious chore, you ask? Fear not, for the art of maintaining a juicer is much like tending to a cherished garden; it requires regular care, a smidgen of patience, and a touch of love.

First and foremost, let's debunk a common myth: cleaning your juicer doesn't necessitate an elaborate ritual. It's more about adopting certain habits and incorporating them into your juicing routine. One of the golden rules is timeliness. The longer you let the remnants sit, the harder they become to remove, as they dry and stick. Make it a practice to clean your juicer immediately after use. Not in an hour, not after dinner, but right then. This simple shift in routine can be the difference between a quick rinse and a scrubbing marathon.

Water, that universal solvent, is your first line of defense. A good initial rinse can dislodge a significant portion of the pulp and residue. For those parts that are dishwasher-safe, a trip through the machine can handle the rest. However, for the more intricate components, especially those in direct contact with fruits and vegetables, a bit more attention is warranted.

Employing a soft brush, much like an artist uses to create intricate details, can work wonders. Gentle, circular motions can effectively clear out the nooks and crannies without causing any wear or tear. Avoid the temptation to use anything abrasive; remember, it's about caressing, not battling the residue.

When it comes to the filter, a crucial component in most juicers, consider it like the heart of the machine. It needs special care. Filters, especially the fine mesh ones, can trap tiny particles. A dedicated brush, often provided with the juicer, or a simple toothbrush can be instrumental in dislodging these particles, ensuring smooth operation and optimal juice quality.

Now, every once in a while, despite your best efforts, you might encounter stubborn stains, especially if you're a fan of vibrant produce like carrots or beets. In such scenarios, natural solutions can be your ally. A mixture of baking soda and water, left to sit on the stain for a few minutes, can gently lift it, restoring the pristine nature of your machine.

Beyond cleaning, regular maintenance ensures longevity. Periodically inspect the various parts of your juicer. Blades and gears, over time, can become dull or worn out. Replacing them not only ensures efficiency but also safety. Rubber components, seals, or gaskets can also degrade. Keeping an eye on them can prevent potential leaks or malfunctions.

While maintenance and cleaning are paramount, there are also a few tips to enhance your overall juicing experience. For instance, alternating between hard and soft produce can naturally help clean the juicer as you use it. The firmness of apples or carrots can push through the softer residues of leafy greens or citrus fruits.

Another nugget of wisdom is to listen to your juicer. Much like an old friend, it communicates. If it starts sounding different, struggling, or vibrating more than usual, it might be time for a checkup. Addressing small issues proactively can prevent bigger, more expensive problems down the road.

The act of juicing is more than a mere blending of fruits and vegetables; it is an intimate dance between nature's bounty and human innovation. The juicer, our faithful partner in this dance, deserves our understanding and diligent care. As we've traversed the diverse landscapes of juicers and their maintenance, it becomes evident that a well-chosen and well-maintained juicer is not just a machine; it's a commitment to a healthier, more vibrant life. Equip yourself wisely and honor the bond you share with this remarkable tool.

Part II: Recipes to Rejuvenate

Chapter 4: Energize Your Mornings: Breakfast Juices

Awaken your senses and bolster your vitality as dawn breaks with an array of delightful juices designed for the early riser. The allure of citrusy concoctions brims with zest, promising to invigorate your mornings. Meanwhile, the symphony of sweet and nutty combinations seamlessly marries indulgence with nutrition. Embrace these liquid harmonies that encompass the spirit of various global cultures, each sip transporting you to a unique culinary landscape.

Citrus Symphony: Bright and Zesty Blends

Recipe 1: Citrus Sunrise Elixir

P.T.: 10 minutes

Ingr.: Merge 2 pink grapefruits, 3 Cara Cara oranges, 1 lemon, a ginger segment measuring about an inch, and optionally, a teaspoon of agave nectar.

Serves: 2

M. of C.: Machine squeezing

Process: Navigate grapefruits, oranges, lemon, and ginger through the machine squeezer. Upon culmination, incorporate agave for a subtle sweetness.

N.V.: This potion provides approximately 180 calories per serving, loaded with 250% of your daily Vitamin C needs, and about 12% of daily potassium. The infusion is an immunity booster, fights inflammation, and aids in promoting good digestive health.

Recipe 2: Lime Luster Splash

P.T.: 7 minutes

Ingr.: Assemble 5 limes, 2 verdant apples, and a cluster of fresh mint leaves.

Serves: 2

M. of C.: Machine squeezing

Process: Propel limes, apples, and mint into the squeezer. Once transformed, serve this invigorating potion chilled.

N.V.: Contains roughly 155 calories, bursting with 220% daily Vitamin C and 8% of dietary fiber, it is designed to enhance skin health, aid in digestion, and refresh your breath.

Recipe 3: Tangerine Tango Twist

P.T.: 8 minutes

Ingr.: Conjoin 4 tangerines, 2 blood oranges, and a dash of cayenne pepper for an adventurous edge.

Serves: 2

M. of C.: Machine squeezing

Process: Employ the machine squeezer to extract the juicy essence of the tangerines and blood oranges. Post extraction, blend in the cayenne to awaken your palate.

N.V.: This delightful blend offers about 170 calories, generously endows you with 240% of daily Vitamin C, and is rich in flavonoid antioxidants. Expect a boost in immune health, enhanced collagen synthesis, and a kickstart to your metabolism.

Recipe 4: Golden Citrus Medley

P.T.: 12 minutes

Ingr.: Harness 3 oranges, 2 golden kiwis, and a segment of turmeric spanning about an inch.

Serves: 2

M. of C.: Machine squeezing

Process: Adjoin oranges, kiwis, and turmeric into the squeezer. Once all components have been adequately juiced, unify the extracts and enjoy.

N.V.: Offering approximately 200 calories, with a bounty of 280% of your daily Vitamin C intake, the infusion is also studded with anti-inflammatory benefits, fostering a hearty immune response and promoting joint health.

Recipe 5: Ruby Grapefruit Glory

P.T.: 10 minutes

Ingr.: Conflate 3 ruby grapefruits and a hint of organic lavender extract.

Serves: 2

M. of C.: Machine squeezing

Process: Entrust grapefruits to the machine squeezer and post extraction, merge in the fragrant lavender touch.

N.V.: Laden with about 180 calories per potion, with 210% daily Vitamin C, it's your heart-friendly concoction, credited for improving good cholesterol and supporting stress relief.

Sweet and Nutty Combinations

Recipe 1: Pecan Praline Pleasure

P.T.: 14 minutes

Ingr.: Entangle 4 ripe bananas, a handful of toasted pecans, and a drizzle of maple syrup.

Serves: 2

M. of C.: Machine squeezing

Process: Escort bananas and pecans into the squeezer. Subsequently, swathe the juice with the maple drizzle to kindle sweetness.

N.V.: Approximately 280 calories, rich in potassium and magnesium. This blend ensures heart health and a sustained energy release.

Recipe 2: Coconut Charm Whisper

P.T.: 16 minutes

Ingr.: Engage 3 ripe mangoes, 1 cup of unsweetened coconut milk, and a touch of cinnamon.

Serves: 2

M. of C.: Machine squeezing

Process: Introduce mangoes into the squeezer. Thereafter, fuse the juice with coconut milk, finishing with a hint of cinnamon.

N.V.: At 300 calories, this potion delivers a healthy dose of Vitamin A and E, promoting radiant skin and robust vision.

Recipe 3: Hazel Harmony Brew

P.T.: 15 minutes

Ingr.: Accumulate 4 figs, a splash of almond milk, and a handful of roasted hazelnuts.

Serves: 2

M. of C.: Machine squeezing

Process: Navigate figs through the squeezer, and later amalgamate with almond milk and a hazelnut infusion.

N.V.: About 240 calories, it's a fiber and calcium-rich concoction, aiding in digestion and bone health.

Recipe 4: Walnut Waltz Elixir

P.T.: 18 minutes

Ingr.: Unite 5 kiwis, a fistful of walnuts, and a dash of honey.

Serves: 2

M. of C.: Machine squeezing

Process: Channel kiwis into the squeezer. Subsequent to extraction, blend the juice with walnuts and a touch of honey.

N.V.: Possessing 250 calories, with abundant Vitamin K and Omega-3, this elixir is adept in brain health and ensures smoother skin.

Recipe 5: Pistachio Poise Potion

P.T.: 17 minutes

Ingr.: Converge 3 ripe pears, a handful of pistachios, and a whisper of vanilla extract.

Serves: 2

M. of C.: Machine squeezing

Process: Shear pears through the squeezer, and in the aftermath, weave the juice with pistachios and the aromatic vanilla essence.

N.V.: Around 270 calories, suffused with Vitamin C and antioxidants, it promises a heightened immune system and antiviral properties.

As the golden rays of the morning sun pierce through the horizon, having a glass filled with these nutritious elixirs ensures a kick-start filled with verve and vigor. Our journey through zesty blends and nutty harmonies imparts not only the allure of flavor but also the promise of wellness. With every gulp, reaffirm your commitment to a day of productivity, health, and sheer culinary joy.

Chapter 5: Weight-Loss Juices that Pack a Punch

Venture into the realm of revitalizing concoctions, meticulously crafted to aid those on their weight-loss odyssey. This chapter is not just about shedding pounds; it's about nourishing the body with intentional ingredients, each possessing its own tale of metabolism-boosting prowess. The world is teeming with an array of vegetables and fruits that not only burst with flavor but also champion weight reduction. By intertwining these ingredients, we curate elixirs that aren't mere drinks but symphonies of health and taste, each note echoing the promise of a lighter, energized self.

Green Goddess: Veggie-Dominant Recipes

Recipe 1: Verdant Vitality Boost

P.T.: 15 minutes

Ingr.: A hearty handful of kale, three elongated celery stalks, two cucumbers (preferably Persian), a modest sprig of mint, and a lone green apple.

Serves: 2

M. of C.: Machine Squeezing

Process: First, ensure the kale's ribs are detached, the cucumbers are gently washed, and the celery is devoid of any leaves. Halve the apple, removing its core. Assemble the ingredients in your juicer in the order presented above, beginning with the kale and culminating with the apple. Engage your machine, letting its power derive the juice. Once finished, intersperse the freshly squeezed elixir with mint leaves, stirring delicately.

N.V.: This blend fortifies the system with vitamin A and vitamin K. The cucumber's inherent hydration properties work harmoniously with celery's detoxifying prowess. The kale proffers calcium, while the apple introduces a subtle sweetness without excessive sugars. The essence of mint not only invigorates the palate but also aids digestion.

Recipe 2: Spinach Soothe

P.T.: 10 minutes

Ingr.: A verdant cluster of spinach, a pair of juicy pears, a ginger segment about the size of a thumbnail, and a squeeze of lemon.

Serves: 2

M. of C.: Machine Squeezing

Process: Commence by cleansing the spinach and pears. Slice the pears into manageable sections, discarding the core. Introduce the spinach into your juicer, followed by the pears, and then incorporate the ginger. Once all ingredients have been juiced, elevate the flavor profile with a hint of lemon.

N.V.: This concoction is a reservoir of iron and magnesium courtesy of spinach. The pears enhance the juice's fiber content, promoting satiety, while the ginger stimulates metabolism and harbors anti-inflammatory properties.

Recipe 3: Broccoli Brilliance

P.T.: 12 minutes

Ingr.: Four broccoli florets, two green apples, half of a lime, and a small chunk of turmeric.

Serves: 2

M. of C.: Machine Squeezing

Process: Initiate the procedure by washing the broccoli florets and the green apples. The apples should be segmented, ensuring the core is excised. Merge the broccoli, apples, lime, and turmeric within your juicer. Once the juice manifests, stir for a uniform consistency.

N.V.: The cruciferous powerhouse, broccoli, offers vitamin C and folate. Green apples, with their quercetin content, act as antioxidants. Lime provides a tangy twist and promotes skin health, while turmeric enhances anti-inflammatory benefits.

Recipe 4: Zucchini Zen

P.T.: 8 minutes

Ingr.: Two medium zucchinis, a handful of parsley, one green bell pepper, and a dash of Himalayan pink salt.

Serves: 2

M. of C.: Machine Squeezing

Process: Embark by cleansing and trimming the zucchinis. Dice the green bell pepper, ensuring the seeds are relegated. Now, unite the zucchinis, parsley, and green bell pepper in your juicer. Upon extraction, elevate the juice with a pinch of Himalayan pink salt.

N.V.: Zucchinis are laden with vitamin B6, contributing to energy metabolism. Parsley is an excellent source of vitamin K, crucial for bone health. Green bell pepper is an antioxidant-rich vegetable, while Himalayan pink salt imparts trace minerals.

Recipe 5: Cabbage Calm

P.T.: 10 minutes

Ingr.: A quarter of a green cabbage, two kiwis, a sprinkle of black pepper, and a wedge of lime.

Serves: 2

M. of C.: Machine Squeezing

Process: Embark by shearing the cabbage into shreds, ensuring its core is discarded. Peel the kiwis, segmenting them into halves. Propagate the shredded cabbage and kiwis into the juicer, and upon complete extraction, accentuate the juice with lime and a hint of black pepper.

N.V.: Cabbage, a dietary fiber dynamo, aids digestion and offers vitamin C. Kiwis, with their actinidin content, foster improved digestion and are teeming with vitamin E. The subtle addition of black pepper stimulates nutrient absorption.

The Light Fruit: Low-Calorie Delights

Recipe 1: Crimson Drizzle

P.T.: 10 minutes

Ingr.: A couple of lush red plums, one watermelon slice (rind removed), a small wedge of lemon, and a sprig of fresh basil.

Serves: 2

M. of C.: Machine Squeezing

Process: Cleanse the plums and halve them, discarding the stones. Feed the plums, watermelon slice, and lemon wedge into the juicer. Once you've coaxed out their liquid essence, stir gently, garnishing with finely chopped basil.

N.V.: This delightful potion carries approximately 68 calories per serving, offering 0.5g protein, 0.3g fat, and 17g carbohydrates. Plums tantalize the taste buds and offer vitamin C, vital for skin health. Watermelon hydrates and presents lycopene. Lemon sparks metabolism, and basil imparts anti-inflammatory properties.

Recipe 2: Peachy Purity

P.T.: 8 minutes

Ingr.: Three sun-ripened peaches, half a cucumber, and a thumb-sized ginger piece.

Serves: 2

M. of C.: Machine Squeezing

Process: Begin by washing the peaches. Slice them into eighths, removing their pits. Introduce the peaches, cucumber, and ginger into the juicer. Once squeezed to satisfaction, swirl the blend to achieve a seamless consistency.

N.V.: Each serving comes with a modest 72 calories, augmented by 1g protein, 0.5g fat, and 18g carbohydrates. Peaches, laden with fiber, promote satiety and offer vitamin A. Cucumber refreshes, while ginger elevates metabolism and provides anti-inflammatory benefits.

Recipe 3: Melon Mélange

P.T.: 10 minutes

Ingr.: Half a honeydew melon (seeds removed), a small bunch of green grapes, and a dash of fresh mint.

Serves: 2

M. of C.: Machine Squeezing

Process: Segment the honeydew into manageable chunks. Transfer the melon pieces and green grapes into the juicer. Upon deriving the juice, infuse it with a touch of mint for an invigorating finish.

N.V.: One serving boasts about 90 calories, complemented by 1.2g protein, 0.4g fat, and 22g carbohydrates. Honeydew melons are a bountiful source of vitamin C and potassium. Green grapes add resveratrol, with heart-healthy benefits. Mint aids in digestion.

Recipe 4: Berry Bliss

P.T.: 12 minutes

Ingr.: A handful of blueberries, a clutch of strawberries, a single lime wedge, and a sprinkle of chia seeds.

Serves: 2

M. of C.: Machine Squeezing

Process: Cleanse the blueberries and strawberries, discarding the strawberry stems. Initiate the juicing with the berries, followed by the lime. Once the essence is derived, enhance with a smattering of chia seeds.

N.V.: A single serving provides roughly 70 calories, 1g protein, 0.7g fat, and 16g carbohydrates. Blueberries and strawberries are antioxidant powerhouses, combating oxidative stress. Lime provides a tart twist and vitamin C, while chia seeds enrich with omega-3 fatty acids.

Recipe 5: Pearlescent Pleasure

P.T.: 10 minutes

Ingr.: Two juicy pears, a single kiwi, a slice of pineapple, and a spritz of lemon.

Serves: 2

M. of C.: Machine Squeezing

Process: Wash and core the pears. Peel the kiwi and pineapple, dicing them appropriately. Initiate your juicing ritual with the pears, then proceed with the kiwi and pineapple. Conclude with a zesty lemon spritz.

N.V.: Enjoying this elixir bestows you with about 95 calories per serving, combined with 1.1g protein, 0.5g fat, and 24g carbohydrates. Pears help maintain digestive regularity. Kiwi improves digestion and is a skin ally, while pineapple aids protein digestion. Lemon not only elevates flavor but also boosts metabolism.

Reflecting on the myriad of recipes unfurled, it's evident that weight-loss isn't just about subtracting but also about adding: adding flavor, nutrition, and vigor. By imbibing these meticulously designed drinks, one doesn't merely embrace a diet but a lifestyle—a harmonious blend of taste and health, of indulgence and discipline. Let each sip be a step towards the finest version of oneself, invigorated and ever-evolving.

Chapter 6: Anti-Ageing Elixirs

Time's passage, a reality we all face, finds its most visible markers on our skin and energy levels. However, nature, in its infinite wisdom, has sprinkled the earth with ingredients brimming with anti-ageing properties. This chapter beckons you to delve into elixirs, woven from these nature's treasures, promising not a retreat from age but a graceful dance with it. These drinks are tales of rejuvenation, where every sip holds the promise of revitalized skin, bolstered vitality, and a radiant glow from within.

Berry Beautiful: Antioxidant-Rich Mixes

Recipe 1: Ruby Radiance

P.T.: 10 minutes

Ingr.: A bounty of blackberries, a cluster of cherries (pitted), a sliver of acai berry pulp, and a hint of rooibos tea.

Serves: 2

M. of C.: Machine Squeezing

Process: Begin by washing the blackberries and cherries thoroughly. Start your juicing process with these vibrant berries and follow with the acai pulp. Once you've captured their essence, blend the juice with a splash of chilled rooibos tea.

N.V.: This elixir brings forth roughly 80 calories per serving, harmonized by 1.5g protein, 0.8g fat, and 18g carbohydrates. Blackberries and cherries offer anthocyanins, fortifying cellular health. Acai, a superfruit, further intensifies the antioxidant profile. Rooibos tea presents a unique blend of minerals and anti-ageing compounds.

Recipe 2: Indigo Infusion

P.T.: 12 minutes

Ingr.: A handful of blueberries, a smattering of elderberries, a shard of dark chocolate (70% cocoa), and a sprinkle of flaxseed powder.

Serves: 2

M. of C.: Machine Squeezing

Process: After cleansing the blueberries and elderberries, initiate your juicing journey. Once their juices meld, introduce a finely grated shard of dark chocolate, stirring fervently. Finalize with a gentle infusion of flaxseed powder.

N.V.: Each serving wields about 90 calories, with 2g protein, 2.5g fat, and 16g carbohydrates. Blueberries bolster brain function, elderberries enhance skin elasticity, dark chocolate provides flavonoids, and flaxseeds grace us with omega-3 fatty acids.

Recipe 3: Scarlet Serenity

P.T.: 8 minutes

Ingr.: A collection of cranberries, a wedge of pomegranate, and a touch of hibiscus extract.

Serves: 2

M. of C.: Machine Squeezing

Process: After thoroughly washing the cranberries, introduce them to the juicer. Extract the gems from the pomegranate and let them dance in next. Upon achieving a seamless juice, harmonize with a few drops of hibiscus extract.

N.V.: Indulgence in this potion grants approximately 85 calories per serving, alongside 1g protein, 0.5g fat, and 21g carbohydrates. Cranberries proffer UT health benefits, pomegranate brings punicalagins and punicic acid for skin rejuvenation, and hibiscus offsets ageing with its vitamin C content.

Recipe 4: Golden Glimmer

P.T.: 10 minutes

Ingr.: A portion of goji berries, a slice of mango, and a piece of turmeric root.

Serves: 2

M. of C.: Machine Squeezing

Process: Submerge goji berries in water briefly to soften them. Alongside, peel and segment the mango. Commence the juicing ritual with goji berries, followed by mango pieces. Integrate a grated piece of fresh turmeric into the elixir.

N.V.: Savoring this blend offers about 100 calories per serving, complemented by 1.5g protein, 1g fat, and 23g carbohydrates. Goji berries, hailed as a superfood, extend zeaxanthin and polysaccharides. Mango, rich in vitamin A, and turmeric, with its curcumin, together amplify the anti-ageing prowess.

Recipe 5: Lavender Luminescence

P.T.: 9 minutes

Ingr.: A cup of grapes (seedless), a sprig of fresh lavender, and a drop of rosehip oil.

Serves: 2

M. of C.: Machine Squeezing

Process: After rinsing grapes, welcome them into the juicer. Once the juice is drawn, whisk in finely chopped lavender and conclude with a solitary drop of rosehip oil, blending till ethereal.

N.V.: This concoction bestows roughly 78 calories per serving, allied with 0.8g protein, 1g fat, and 19g carbohydrates. Grapes are replete with resveratrol, countering skin ageing. Lavender soothes, and rosehip oil, a carrier of vitamin C and E, contributes to skin hydration and elasticity.

Rooted in Youth: Vegetable Blends

Recipe 1: Amber Ambrosia

P.T.: 10 minutes

Ingr.: A cluster of carrots, a snippet of ginger root, and a touch of beetroot.

Serves: 2

M. of C.: Machine Squeezing

Process: Wash and peel the carrots and beetroot. Slice them into manageable pieces. Take a ginger piece and grate it finely. First, run the carrots through the juicer, followed by the beetroot. Finally, sprinkle in the ginger gratings and give it a gentle stir.

N.V.: Delving into this tonic rewards around 95 calories per serving, accompanying 2g protein, 0.5g fat, and 22g carbohydrates. Carrots, bountiful in beta-carotene, invigorate eye health. Ginger contains gingerol, aiding skin health, and beetroot is a vascular health enhancer.

Recipe 2: Emerald Euphoria

P.T.: 12 minutes

Ingr.: An array of spinach leaves, a fragment of avocado, and a dollop of celery stalks.

Serves: 2

M. of C.: Machine Squeezing

Process: Thoroughly wash spinach leaves and celery. Dice the avocado, discarding its seed. Introduce spinach and celery to the juicer, later integrating the avocado puree for a creamy, smooth finish.

N.V.: This concoction offers about 110 calories per serving, inclusive of 3g protein, 7g fat, and 9g carbohydrates. Spinach, being vitamin C enriched, fortifies the skin. Avocado offers skin-moisturizing fats, while celery brings in skin-clearing antioxidants.

Recipe 3: Sienna Serendipity

P.T.: 10 minutes

Ingr.: A bundle of sweet potatoes, a sliver of cinnamon bark, and a touch of parsnip.

Serves: 2

M. of C.: Machine Squeezing

Process: Clean and peel sweet potatoes and parsnip, cutting them into chunks. Pass them through the juicer. Once you've acquired their velvety juice, season with a hint of cinnamon powder.

N.V.: Sipping on this potion gives approximately 120 calories per serving, alongside 2.5g protein, 0.4g fat, and 28g carbohydrates. Sweet potatoes provide a vitamin A punch, countering skin ageing. Parsnip enriches with fiber and antioxidants, while cinnamon offers anti-inflammatory properties.

Recipe 4: Peridot Pleasure

P.T.: 15 minutes
Ingr.: A portion of broccoli florets, a segment of fennel bulb, and a slice of lime.
Serves: 2
M. of C.: Machine Squeezing
Process: Wash broccoli and fennel meticulously. Segment them for juicing ease. Juice them in succession, and end with a squeeze of fresh lime, ensuring its citrusy charm melds seamlessly.

N.V.: Partaking in this blend bestows around 70 calories per serving, complemented by 4g protein, 0.5g fat, and 16g carbohydrates. Broccoli offers sulforaphane, a skin-protecting compound. Fennel promotes digestion and detox, and lime invigorates with its vitamin C profile.

Recipe 5: Jade Jubilation

P.T.: 9 minutes
Ingr.: A heap of kale leaves, a chunk of cucumber, and a pinch of fresh mint.
Serves: 2
M. of C.: Machine Squeezing
Process: After a thorough wash of kale, cucumber, and mint, chop them for juicing convenience. Begin with the kale, succeeding with cucumber, and finalize with mint leaves, ensuring an aromatic blend.

N.V.: This elixir grants roughly 60 calories per serving, allied with 3g protein, 0.3g fat, and 14g carbohydrates. Kale, a vitamin K reservoir, promotes skin healing. Cucumber hydrates and cools, while mint rejuvenates with its menthol essence.

As our journey through these age-defying potions concludes, we're reminded of the power of nature and its ability to heal, nurture, and renew. In these beverages lies not a promise of eternal youth but a pledge of ageless grace. By embracing these natural concoctions, we don't defy time but rather celebrate it, ensuring each passing moment is as vibrant as the last.

Part III: Speciality Juicing

Chapter 7: Detox and Cleanse: Purifying Mixes

The daily hustle and bustling city life often leave our bodies yearning for a clean slate, a reset button. Detoxifying isn't just a fancy term; it's an invitation to purity and revitalization, allowing our systems to shed accumulated toxins and embrace a feeling of rejuvenation. As you navigate through these pages, you'll encounter the gentle magic of Liver Lovables and feel the renewing touch of hydrating blends that cater to both your palate and well-being. In the alchemy of juicing, the art isn't just in the blend but in understanding the profound transformations these mixes gift to our bodies.

Liver Lovables: Gentle Detoxifiers

Recipe 1: Verdant Vitalizer

P.T.: 10 minutes

Ingr.: A handful of dandelion greens, three medium carrots, one beetroot, half a fresh lemon (peeled), a small piece of ginger (about an inch), and one tablespoon of cold-pressed flaxseed oil.

Serves: 2

M. of C.: Machine squeezing

Process: Begin by washing all the vegetables thoroughly. Once cleaned, peel the beetroot and ginger. Trim the dandelion greens and carrots. Place everything into the juicer, starting with the dandelion greens, followed by the carrots, beetroot, ginger, and ending with the lemon. Once juiced, stir in the cold-pressed flaxseed oil to ensure a uniform blend. Serve chilled.

N.V.: Calories: 115, Protein: 2.5g, Fat: 4.5g, Carbohydrates: 18g. This juice is a rich source of vitamin A, essential for liver health, and detoxifying compounds from the dandelion greens.

Recipe 2: Turmeric Tonic

P.T.: 8 minutes

Ingr.: Two green apples, one cucumber, half a lemon, two inches of fresh turmeric root, and a pinch of black pepper.

Serves: 2

M. of C.: Machine squeezing

Process: After washing the fruits and veggies, peel the lemon and turmeric root. Juice the green apples followed by the cucumber, turmeric, and lemon. Stir in a pinch of black pepper which can enhance the absorption of curcumin from the turmeric. Enjoy immediately.

N.V.: Calories: 90, Protein: 1g, Fat: 0.5g, Carbohydrates: 22g. Turmeric has renowned anti-inflammatory properties and aids in liver detoxification.

Recipe 3: Minty Beet Bliss

P.T.: 12 minutes

Ingr.: Two medium-sized beetroots, a bunch of mint leaves, one carrot, half a pineapple, and a pinch of Himalayan pink salt.

Serves: 2-3

M. of C.: Machine squeezing

Process: Clean all ingredients. Peel the beetroots and carrot. Slice the pineapple into manageable pieces. Begin juicing with the mint, then add the beetroots, carrot, and pineapple. Once all are juiced, stir in the pink salt for a slight savory touch.

N.V.: Calories: 110, Protein: 2g, Fat: 0.7g, Carbohydrates: 26g. Beetroot contains betaine, aiding liver function and detoxification.

Recipe 4: Gingered Green Glory

P.T.: 10 minutes

Ingr.: A handful of spinach, two green apples, one celery stalk, two inches of ginger root, and one lime.

Serves: 2

M. of C.: Machine squeezing

Process: After thorough washing, start juicing with the spinach, followed by the apples, celery, ginger, and finishing with the lime. Serve immediately for a refreshing detox drink.

N.V.: Calories: 95, Protein: 1.5g, Fat: 0.4g, Carbohydrates: 24g. Ginger promotes digestion, helps in detoxification, and boasts anti-inflammatory properties.

Recipe 5: Cilantro Citrus Cleaner

P.T.: 7 minutes

Ingr.: A bunch of fresh cilantro, one grapefruit, two oranges, and a teaspoon of chia seeds.

Serves: 2

M. of C.: Machine squeezing

Process: Clean the cilantro properly. Peel the grapefruit and oranges, ensuring to remove all seeds. Juice the cilantro first, followed by the citrus fruits. Pour into glasses and stir in chia seeds for an added nutritional boost.

N.V.: Calories: 120, Protein: 2g, Fat: 2g, Carbohydrates: 25g. Cilantro is known for its heavy metal detoxifying properties, making this juice a potent cleanser.

Refresh and Reset: Hydrating Blends

Recipe 1: Cucumber Cascade

P.T.: 5 minutes

Ingr.: Two large cucumbers, half a lime, a sprig of rosemary, and a pinch of sea salt.

Serves: 2

M. of C.: Machine squeezing

Process: Begin by washing the cucumbers and lime. Peel the lime. Juice the cucumbers first, allowing their high water content to hydrate your blend, then add the lime. Once ready, pour into glasses, adding a pinch of sea salt and garnishing with rosemary.

N.V.: Calories: 30, Protein: 1g, Fat: 0.2g, Carbohydrates: 6g. Cucumbers are 95% water, making them an ideal base for a hydrating concoction.

Recipe 2: Watermelon Wave

P.T.: 7 minutes

Ingr.: Half a small watermelon, a handful of fresh basil leaves, and one teaspoon of aloe vera gel.

Serves: 2-3

M. of C.: Machine squeezing

Process: Scoop out the flesh of the watermelon after discarding seeds. Juice the watermelon chunks, followed by the basil leaves. Stir in the aloe vera gel post juicing for a soothing touch.

N.V.: Calories: 60, Protein: 1g, Fat: 0.3g, Carbohydrates: 15g. Aloe vera enhances hydration and soothes the digestive system.

Recipe 3: Pineapple Pacific

P.T.: 10 minutes

Ingr.: Half a pineapple, one stalk of celery, half a cucumber, and a pinch of cayenne pepper.

Serves: 2

M. of C.: Machine squeezing

Process: Slice the pineapple into sections, discarding the core. Juice the pineapple, followed by the celery and cucumber. Sprinkle in a touch of cayenne for a zesty kick.

N.V.: Calories: 90, Protein: 1g, Fat: 0.2g, Carbohydrates: 22g. Pineapple contains bromelain which aids digestion.

Recipe 4: Coconut Bliss Burst

P.T.: 8 minutes

Ingr.: Meat from one young coconut, one cup of coconut water, a small bunch of mint leaves, and a slice of lemon.

Serves: 2

M. of C.: Machine squeezing

Process: Extract the meat from the young coconut and set the water aside. Juice the coconut meat along with mint leaves. Mix this juice with the reserved coconut water and squeeze in fresh lemon.

N.V.: Calories: 80, Protein: 2g, Fat: 4g, Carbohydrates: 9g. Coconut provides essential electrolytes, ensuring you remain hydrated.

Recipe 5: Ginger Green Quench

P.T.: 6 minutes

Ingr.: Two green apples, a fistful of kale, two inches of ginger root, and one cup of sparkling water.

Serves: 2

M. of C.: Machine squeezing

Process: Wash the apples and kale. Juice them along with the ginger root. Pour this mixture into glasses and top up with sparkling water for a fizzy finish.

N.V.: Calories: 85, Protein: 1.5g, Fat: 0.3g, Carbohydrates: 20g. Kale, rich in vitamins, pairs with ginger's anti-inflammatory properties for a rejuvenating drink.

As the final drops of these purifying concoctions glide down your throat, a sense of serenity and lightness might just wash over you. Our journey through detoxification and cleansing with these special recipes has been about embracing health, honoring our bodies, and connecting with the purest versions of ourselves. It's a delightful dance of flavors and wellness, one that redefines the relationship between nourishment and purity. Allow these juices to be your gentle reminders of self-care in a glass, urging you to periodically pause, cleanse, and reset.

Chapter 8: Wellness Shots and Immunity Boosters

In a world where daily routines are inundated with stressors, both physical and mental, fortifying our body becomes imperative. This chapter delves into the elixirs of health and vitality, condensed into shots packed with nutrition. It's about harnessing the power of potent pots and intertwining the age-old wisdom of herbs to provide a daily boost. Nature's apothecary, brimming with herbs and potent ingredients, stands ready to arm you against the ebb and flow of daily challenges.

Potent Pots: Condensed Nutrition

Recipe 1: Golden Elixir Surge

P.T.: 10 minutes

Ingr.: 1-inch piece fresh turmeric, peeled; 1-inch piece fresh ginger, peeled; 2 black peppercorns; Half a lemon, peeled; 1 teaspoon raw honey; A pinch of Himalayan pink salt.

Serves: 2

M. of C.: Machine squeezing

Process: Start by washing all the fresh ingredients thoroughly under running water. Once cleaned, chop the turmeric and ginger into small pieces to facilitate easy extraction. In a juicer, introduce turmeric, ginger, and the lemon. Process until you obtain a smooth liquid. Pour this extraction into a small container. Grind the black peppercorns and sprinkle them into the mix. Stir in the raw honey and the pinch of Himalayan pink salt until well combined. Serve in shot glasses, ensuring each serving has an equal blend of the ingredients.

N.V.: Calories: 40; Protein: 0.3g; Fat: 0.1g; Carbohydrates: 10g. The combination of turmeric and black pepper boosts curcumin absorption, potentially offering anti-inflammatory effects and enhancing immunity. Ginger brings in its anti-nausea and digestive benefits. The addition of lemon provides a shot of vitamin C, while honey acts as a natural sweetener with its own range of health benefits.

Recipe 2: Spirulina Powerhouse

P.T.: 7 minutes

Ingr.: 2 teaspoons of Spirulina powder; 1 small cucumber; Half a green apple; 1 stalk celery; A splash of coconut water.

Serves: 2

M. of C.: Machine squeezing

Process: Ensure all the ingredients, especially the fresh ones, are cleaned properly. Slice the cucumber, green apple, and celery into pieces that are manageable for the juicer. Initiate the juicing process by first introducing the cucumber, then the green apple, and finally the celery stalk. Once juiced, mix in the Spirulina powder and stir vigorously to ensure there are no clumps. Add a splash of coconut water for a tropical twist and enhanced hydration.

N.V.: Calories: 50; Protein: 2.5g; Fat: 0.2g; Carbohydrates: 12g. Spirulina is a potent source of nutrients, antioxidants, and both Vitamin B1 and Iron. The celery offers digestive benefits, while the cucumber and green apple offer hydration and a mild sweetness, respectively. Coconut water enriches the shot with electrolytes.

Recipe 3: Beetroot Vitality Vial

P.T.: 10 minutes

Ingr.: 1 medium-sized beetroot, peeled; 1 carrot; Half an orange, peeled; A pinch of cayenne pepper; 1 teaspoon of chia seeds.

Serves: 2

M. of C.: Machine squeezing

Process: Firstly, cleanse all fresh components meticulously. Slice the beetroot and carrot into juicer-friendly pieces. Start the juicing with beetroot, followed by carrot and then the orange half. Once you've obtained the juice, introduce a pinch of cayenne pepper for a slight kick. Stir well. Before serving, sprinkle chia seeds atop the shot for a crunch and let it sit for a couple of minutes to allow the seeds to swell.

N.V.: Calories: 60; Protein: 1.2g; Fat: 0.4g; Carbohydrates: 14g. Beetroot is renowned for its ability to enhance stamina, thanks to dietary nitrates. The carrot adds beta-carotene, beneficial for vision, while the orange offers a vitamin C boost. Cayenne pepper might boost metabolism, and chia seeds bring in omega-3 fatty acids.

Recipe 4: Pineapple Paradigm Punch

P.T.: 8 minutes

Ingr.: A slice of ripe pineapple; 1 teaspoon of ground turmeric; A sprig of mint; A hint of black salt; Half a lime.

Serves: 2

M. of C.: Machine squeezing

Process: Cleanse the pineapple slice and mint sprig thoroughly. Extract juice from the pineapple slice using the machine. To the extracted juice, sprinkle the ground turmeric and squeeze in the juice from half a lime. Mix until well combined. Upon serving, garnish with mint and a hint of black salt for an exotic twist.

N.V.: Calories: 45; Protein: 0.5g; Fat: 0.1g; Carbohydrates: 11g. Pineapple is abundant in bromelain, which can act as a digestive enzyme. Turmeric has potential anti-inflammatory properties, and lime enriches with vitamin C. Mint can potentially soothe the digestive tract, and black salt adds a trace mineral touch.

Recipe 5: Moringa Morning Motivator

P.T.: 7 minutes

Ingr.: 1 teaspoon of Moringa powder; Half a green apple; 1 kiwi, peeled; A splash of aloe vera juice.

Serves: 2

M. of C.: Machine squeezing

Process: After a meticulous cleanse of the apple and kiwi, slice them for juicing. Process the green apple and kiwi through the juicer. To the obtained juice, integrate the Moringa powder. Stir vigorously to ensure no powder clumps remain. Complete the concoction with a splash of aloe vera juice for a soothing touch.

N.V.: Calories: 55; Protein: 1g; Fat: 0.3g; Carbohydrates: 13g. Moringa is dubbed the 'drumstick tree' and is a nutrient-dense powerhouse. Green apple offers a mild sweetness and fiber, kiwi brings in vitamin C and enzymes, and aloe vera juice can potentially aid digestion.

Herbal Harmonies: Incorporating Fresh Herbs

Recipe 1: Basil Bliss Boost

P.T.: 8 minutes

Ingr.: A handful of fresh basil leaves; Half a cucumber; 1 green apple; A touch of pink Himalayan salt; 1 teaspoon of honey.

Serves: 2

M. of C.: Machine squeezing

Process: Begin by washing the basil leaves, cucumber, and green apple. Slice them into manageable pieces suitable for the juicer. First, juice the cucumber followed by the green apple. Once these are processed, add the basil leaves to the juicer. Combine the resulting juice, add a touch of pink Himalayan salt, and then sweeten the mixture with a teaspoon of honey. Give it a thorough stir until the honey dissolves.

N.V.: Calories: 65; Protein: 0.8g; Fat: 0.2g; Carbohydrates: 16g. Basil is not only aromatic but also carries potential anti-inflammatory properties. Cucumber is known for its hydrating qualities, while the green apple provides a hint of tartness and fiber. The honey adds sweetness and antioxidants.

Recipe 2: Minty Melon Elixir

P.T.: 9 minutes

Ingr.: A slice of watermelon; 10 fresh mint leaves; Half a lime; A pinch of ginger powder.

Serves: 2

M. of C.: Machine squeezing

Process: After washing the mint leaves, set them aside. Slice the watermelon into juicer-friendly chunks, ensuring to discard the seeds. Juice the watermelon pieces, then add the mint leaves to the juicer. Squeeze in the juice from half a lime and introduce a pinch of ginger powder. Stir the mixture well to combine.

N.V.: Calories: 50; Protein: 1g; Fat: 0.3g; Carbohydrates: 12g. Watermelon is a delightful source of hydration, while mint can potentially aid in digestion. Lime offers a burst of vitamin C, and ginger powder can be soothing for the stomach.

Recipe 3: Thyme Thrive Tonic

P.T.: 7 minutes

Ingr.: 6-7 sprigs of fresh thyme; 1 pear; Half a lemon; A sprinkle of black pepper.

Serves: 2

M. of C.: Machine squeezing

Process: Cleanse the thyme sprigs and pear thoroughly. Slice the pear into segments fitting for the juicer. Extract juice from the pear slices and then add the thyme sprigs for juicing. To the amalgamated juice, squeeze in the lemon juice and sprinkle a hint of black pepper. Stir briskly for an even blend.

N.V.: Calories: 70; Protein: 0.7g; Fat: 0.2g; Carbohydrates: 17g. Thyme, with its aromatic essence, carries potential antibacterial properties. Pear is a source of fiber and mild sweetness, lemon enriches the mix with vitamin C, and black pepper might boost nutrient absorption.

Recipe 4: Rosemary Radiance Refresher

P.T.: 10 minutes

Ingr.: 2 sprigs of fresh rosemary; 2 oranges, peeled; A touch of cinnamon powder; 1 teaspoon agave syrup.

Serves: 2

M. of C.: Machine squeezing

Process: After cleansing the rosemary sprigs, set them aside. Process the peeled oranges through the juicer. Once juiced, add the rosemary sprigs. After acquiring the juice, season it with a touch of cinnamon powder and sweeten using agave syrup. Stir until well-mingled.

N.V.: Calories: 90; Protein: 1.3g; Fat: 0.3g; Carbohydrates: 22g. Rosemary is believed to enhance memory and concentration. Oranges, bursting with vitamin C, also add natural sweetness. Cinnamon offers warmth and potential blood-sugar stabilizing benefits, while agave provides a vegan-friendly sweetness.

Recipe 5: Lavender Love Liqueur

P.T.: 12 minutes

Ingr.: 1 teaspoon of dried lavender flowers; 1 grapefruit, peeled; A splash of pomegranate juice; 1 teaspoon maple syrup.

Serves: 2

M. of C.: Machine squeezing

Process: Begin by juicing the peeled grapefruit. To the extracted juice, infuse it with dried lavender flowers, allowing it to steep for about 10 minutes. After steeping, strain the liquid to remove the flowers. Add a splash of pomegranate juice for a touch of tartness and color. Sweeten the concoction with maple syrup and stir well.

N.V.: Calories: 95; Protein: 1g; Fat: 0.2g; Carbohydrates: 23g. Lavender, often associated with relaxation and calmness, adds a fragrant twist. Grapefruit can potentially boost metabolism, while pomegranate is packed with antioxidants. Maple syrup lends a gentle, earthy sweetness.

As we journeyed through these powerful concoctions, it's evident that wellness doesn't always require a grand gesture. Sometimes, it's the simplicity of a herb-infused shot or a nutrient-packed beverage that does the trick. The synergy of fresh herbs with fruits and vegetables not only uplifts the palate but also fortifies the body's defenses. May these recipes serve as your shield and tonic, ensuring that every morning you're equipped to face the world with zest and zeal.

Chapter 9: Flavor Adventures with Spices and Exotic Fruits

Journeying into the realms of flavor often requires a spirited explorer to venture beyond the familiar. Across the globe, exotic fruits wait to be discovered, each offering an orchestra of unfamiliar notes, ready to tantalize the palate. Meanwhile, spices, those age-old culinary magicians, enhance and elevate, introducing our senses to new horizons of taste. Together, fruits and spices combine, creating symphonies of flavors that are both intriguing and invigorating.

Tropical Treasures: Exotic Fruit Combinations

Recipe 1: Mangosteen Marvel

P.T.: 10 minutes

Ingr.: Combine 2 cups of peeled and deseeded mangosteen with 1 cup of passion fruit pulp, 1 cup of peeled and pitted lychee, a splash of coconut water, and a hint of lime zest for garnish.

Serves: 2-3

M. of C.: Machine squeezing

Process: Start by ensuring all fruits are thoroughly washed and prepared. Pour mangosteen, passion fruit pulp, and lychees into a juicer and process until smooth. Pour the mixture into glasses, adding a splash of coconut water for a tropical hint. Garnish with lime zest to enhance flavors.

N.V.: Cal: 150, Protein: 2g, Fat: 1g, Carbs: 38g.

Recipe 2: Durian Delight

P.T.: 15 minutes

Ingr.: Mix 1 cup of durian pulp with 1 cup of pineapple chunks, 1 cup of papaya slices, ½ cup of freshly squeezed orange juice, and sprinkle with chia seeds.

Serves: 2-3

M. of C.: Machine squeezing

Process: Extract pulp from durian, ensuring no seeds. In a juicer, blend durian pulp, pineapple, and papaya. Add the orange juice for a citrus contrast. Sprinkle with chia seeds before serving.

N.V.: Cal: 175, Protein: 3g, Fat: 4g, Carbs: 40g.

Recipe 3: Rambutan Reverie

P.T.: 10 minutes

Ingr.: A blend of 2 cups of peeled and pitted rambutan with 1 cup of kiwi chunks and 1 cup of starfruit slices, enhanced with ½ cup of sparkling water and garnished with fresh mint leaves.

Serves: 2

M. of C.: Machine squeezing

Process: Blend rambutan, kiwi, and starfruit in a juicer. Pour the juice into glasses and top up with sparkling water for a bubbly touch. Garnish with fresh mint leaves.

N.V.: Cal: 140, Protein: 2g, Fat: 0.5g, Carbs: 35g.

Recipe 4: Jackfruit Jubilation

P.T.: 12 minutes

Ingr.: Combine 2 cups of jackfruit pods with 1 cup of guava slices, enhance with 2 tablespoons of freshly squeezed lemon juice and a touch of pink Himalayan salt.

Serves: 2-3

M. of C.: Machine squeezing

Process: Mix jackfruit and guava slices in a juicer. After obtaining a smooth blend, add lemon juice and a touch of pink Himalayan salt.

N.V.: Cal: 160, Protein: 3g, Fat: 1g, Carbs: 38g.

Recipe 5: Carambola Concoction

P.T.: 8 minutes

Ingr.: Blend 2 sliced carambola (Starfruit) with 1 cup of dragon fruit chunks, complement with ½ cup of freshly squeezed grapefruit juice, and optionally sweeten with honey or agave syrup.

Serves: 2

M. of C.: Machine squeezing

Process: Incorporate carambola and dragon fruit chunks into the juicer. Once blended, mix in the grapefruit juice. Sweeten to taste.

N.V.: Cal: 130, Protein: 2g, Fat: 0.3g, Carbs: 32g.

Spice Carousel: Adding Zing and Benefits

Recipe 1: Clove & Cranberry Cooler

P.T.: 12 minutes

Ingr.: A harmonious blend of 2 cups cranberry juice, 4-5 whole cloves for a spicy kick, a splash of lime juice, and a touch of agave nectar for added sweetness.

Serves: 2-3

M. of C.: Infusion

Process: First, extract fresh juice from cranberries. Pour the cranberry juice into a pot and bring to a gentle simmer. Add whole cloves, allowing them to infuse their aromatic essence into the juice for about 8 minutes.

Remove from heat and let it cool. Once cooled, add a dash of lime juice and agave nectar to taste. Strain the juice to remove cloves and serve chilled.

N.V.: Cal: 130, Protein: 0.4g, Fat: 0.2g, Carbs: 32g.

Recipe 2: Cinnamon Sunrise

P.T.: 12 minutes

Ingr.: Blend 2 cups of apple juice, a pinch of ground cinnamon, ½ teaspoon of vanilla extract, and a sprinkle of ground nutmeg.

Serves: 2-3

M. of C.: Machine squeezing

Process: Juice fresh apples to achieve the apple juice. Stir in the ground cinnamon, vanilla extract, and a hint of nutmeg for a spiced twist.

N.V.: Cal: 135, Protein: 0.3g, Fat: 0.2g, Carbs: 34g.

Recipe 3: Peppered Pineapple

P.T.: 10 minutes

Ingr.: Mingle 2 cups of pineapple juice, a dash of cayenne pepper, and a sprinkle of pink Himalayan salt.

Serves: 2

M. of C.: Machine squeezing

Process: Juice fresh pineapples until you have your desired amount. Mix in the cayenne pepper and sprinkle the salt. The spiciness from the pepper contrasts beautifully with the sweetness of the pineapple.

N.V.: Cal: 120, Protein: 1g, Fat: 0.1g, Carbs: 30g.

Recipe 4: Cardamom Citrus Fusion

P.T.: 8 minutes

Ingr.: A combination of 2 cups of orange juice, a hint of freshly ground cardamom, a splash of lemon juice, and a sprinkle of zest from an orange peel.

Serves: 2

M. of C.: Machine squeezing

Process: Extract juice from oranges, mix with freshly squeezed lemon juice, stir in the cardamom, and finish with orange zest for an aromatic experience.

N.V.: Cal: 140, Protein: 2g, Fat: 0.3g, Carbs: 33g.

Recipe 5: Star Anise Apple Aid

P.T.: 15 minutes

Ingr.: A mix of 2 cups of apple juice, 1 star anise pod for a licorice hint, a stick of

cinnamon, and a spoon of maple syrup to sweeten.

Serves: 2-3

M. of C.: Infusion

Process: Juice fresh apples to gain apple juice. In a pot, add the apple juice, star anise, and cinnamon stick. Simmer for 10 minutes allowing the spices to infuse. Remove from heat, add maple syrup, strain, and serve warm or cold.

N.V.: Cal: 137, Protein: 0.2g, Fat: 0.3g, Carbs: 35g.

As we wrap up this flavorful expedition, it's evident that combining the richness of spices with the freshness of exotic fruits can transform a simple juice into a global experience. It's not merely about nutrition or hydration; it's a celebration of cultures, tastes, and traditions. As you experiment and adapt, remember that each sip is a step into a vast world of flavors waiting to be discovered.

Part IV: Beyond the Juice

Chapter 10: Meal Replacement and Snack Juices

Venture into a realm where juices and blends aren't just drinks, but satiating meals and delightful snacks. Whether you're on a tight schedule and need a meal-on-the-go or have a sweet craving you don't want to regret later, these concoctions will surely satisfy. Meticulously crafted, these juices are not mere refreshments; they're sustenance, they're treats, they're moments of indulgence without the guilt. Embark on this flavorful journey that marries nutrition with convenience and pleasure.

Hearty Blends: Filling and Nutritious

Recipe 1: Avocado Almond Symphony

P.T.: 10 minutes

Ingr.: A ripe avocado, 1 cup unsweetened almond milk, 2 tsp chia seeds, 1 tsp pure vanilla extract, a smidgeon of honey or agave syrup for sweetness, and a sprinkle of Himalayan pink salt.

Serves: 2

M. of C.: Machine squeezing and blending

Process: Commence by halving the avocado and extracting the pit. With gentle scoops, transfer the avocado flesh into a blender. Pour the almond milk, followed by vanilla extract, chia seeds, and your chosen sweetener. Blend until the mixture reaches a lush, creamy consistency. For a finishing touch, add a sprinkle of Himalayan pink salt and give it one final blend. Pour into glasses and serve immediately.

N.V.: Calories: 210, Protein: 4g, Fat: 16g, Carbs: 12g.

Recipe 2: Berry Oat Odyssey

P.T.: 15 minutes

Ingr.: 1/2 cup rolled oats, a handful of mixed berries (blueberries, raspberries, strawberries), 1 cup unsweetened soy milk, 1 tbsp flax seeds, a hint of cinnamon, and 1 tsp maple syrup.

Serves: 2

M. of C.: Blending

Process: Kick off by soaking the rolled oats in water for about 10 minutes. Drain the water and introduce the soaked oats into a blender. Add the berries, soy milk, flax seeds, cinnamon, and maple syrup. Blend until smooth. Serve in tall glasses for a hearty treat.

N.V.: Calories: 185, Protein: 7g, Fat: 4g, Carbs: 32g.

Recipe 3: Nut Butter Bliss

P.T.: 8 minutes

Ingr.: 1 banana, 2 tbsp almond butter, 1 cup coconut milk, a dash of nutmeg, and 1 tsp cacao nibs.

Serves: 2

M. of C.: Blending

Process: Start by peeling and slicing the banana into manageable chunks. Deposit these into a blender, followed by almond butter, coconut milk, and nutmeg. Whiz until you get a silky mixture. Garnish with cacao nibs before relishing.

N.V.: Calories: 295, Protein: 5g, Fat: 21g, Carbs: 23g.

Recipe 4: Green Grain Galore

P.T.: 12 minutes

Ingr.: 1/2 cup quinoa (cooked), a handful of spinach leaves, 1 apple (cored and sliced), 1 cup oat milk, 1 tbsp pumpkin seeds, and a dribble of agave syrup.

Serves: 2

M. of C.: Blending

Process: Incorporate the cooked quinoa, spinach, apple slices, and oat milk into a blender. Blend till well-mixed. Enhance with pumpkin seeds and agave syrup. One last blend and you're ready to pour and enjoy.

N.V.: Calories: 220, Protein: 6g, Fat: 4g, Carbs: 40g.

Recipe 5: Choco-Chia Dream

P.T.: 10 minutes plus chilling time

Ingr.: 2 tbsp chia seeds, 1.5 cups almond milk, 2 tsp unsweetened cocoa powder, a dash of vanilla essence, and a bit of stevia for sweetness.

Serves: 2

M. of C.: Mixing and chilling

Process: In a mixing bowl, combine chia seeds, cocoa powder, vanilla essence, and almond milk. Whisk well, ensuring no lumps remain. Sweeten with stevia. Let the concoction chill in the fridge for 2-3 hours. Serve cold.

N.V.: Calories: 140, Protein: 5g, Fat: 9g, Carbs: 12g.

Dessert in a Glass: Guilt-Free Pleasures

Recipe 1: Cocoa Coconut Creaminess

P.T.: 10 minutes

Ingr.: 1 cup light coconut milk, 2 tsp unsweetened cocoa powder, a hint of stevia or monk fruit sweetener, 1/2 tsp vanilla essence, a sprinkle of desiccated coconut for garnish.

Serves: 2

M. of C.: Blending

Process: Merge coconut milk, cocoa powder, sweetener, and vanilla essence in a blender. Whirl until you achieve a velvety texture. Pour into glasses and top with desiccated coconut.

N.V.: Calories: 110, Protein: 1g, Fat: 8g, Carbs: 7g.

Recipe 2: Mango Mousse Magic

P.T.: 8 minutes

Ingr.: Flesh of 1 ripe mango, 1/2 cup Greek yogurt, a squeeze of fresh lime, a dash of honey, and mint leaves for garnish.

Serves: 2

M. of C.: Blending

Process: Deposit mango flesh, Greek yogurt, lime, and honey into a blender. Blend till it's utterly creamy. Serve chilled with mint leaf garnish.

N.V.: Calories: 150, Protein: 5g, Fat: 1g, Carbs: 32g.

Recipe 3: Berrylicious Pudding Punch

P.T.: 10 minutes plus chilling time

Ingr.: 1 cup mixed berries (strawberries, blueberries, raspberries), 1/2 cup almond milk, 2 tsp chia seeds, a smidgen of maple syrup, and a touch of vanilla essence.

Serves: 2

M. of C.: Mixing and chilling

Process: Combine berries, almond milk, chia seeds, maple syrup, and vanilla in a bowl. Stir well and let it refrigerate for 3 hours until it takes on a pudding-like consistency. Serve cold.

N.V.: Calories: 125, Protein: 3g, Fat: 4g, Carbs: 20g.

Recipe 4: Caramel Apple Euphoria

P.T.: 12 minutes

Ingr.: 1 apple (cored and chopped), 1 cup unsweetened soy milk, 2 tsp natural almond butter, a drizzle of date syrup, and a sprinkle of cinnamon.

Serves: 2

M. of C.: Blending

Process: Introduce apple pieces, soy milk, almond butter, and date syrup into a blender. Blend until smooth. Add a sprinkle of cinnamon for a spicy kick. Pour and serve immediately.

N.V.: Calories: 185, Protein: 6g, Fat: 7g, Carbs: 25g.

Recipe 5: Creamy Kiwi Concoction

P.T.: 8 minutes

Ingr.: 2 ripe kiwis (peeled and chopped), 1/2 cup coconut yogurt, a drop of honey, and a touch of lime zest.

Serves: 2

M. of C.: Blending

Process: Combine kiwi chunks, coconut yogurt, honey, and lime zest in a blender. Whiz until creamy. Transfer to glasses and serve chilled.

N.V.: Calories: 110, Protein: 2g, Fat: 3g, Carbs: 20g.

And there we have it, a symphony of flavors, each one promising more than just taste - a promise of fullness, of nutrition, and most importantly, of joy. By choosing these juices, you aren't just picking a drink; you're selecting an experience. Whether it's the hearty blends that fill you up or the dessert juices that sweeten your palate, every sip is a step towards holistic wellness and pure enjoyment.

Chapter 11: Incorporating Juices into Meals

The power of juices extends beyond the realm of standalone drinks. In the heart of many cultures, juices have found their way into an array of culinary wonders, serving as the backbone of flavors or as enhancers that elevate a dish from ordinary to extraordinary. Imagine the tangy burst of citrus in a dressing or the sweet reduction of a fruit juice giving life to a savory dish. This section is dedicated to those who are ready to take their culinary ventures a step further by integrating the goodness of juices into sumptuous meals.

Salad Dressings: Zesty and Nutrient-Packed

Recipe 1: Mango Basil Vinaigrette

P.T.: 10 minutes

Ingr.: Fresh mango pulp (from 1 ripe mango), 5 fresh basil leaves finely chopped, 1 tablespoon fresh lime juice, 1 tablespoon apple cider vinegar, 3 tablespoons extra virgin olive oil (EVOO), salt to taste, and a pinch of freshly ground black pepper.

Serves: 4-6

M. of C.: Blending

Process: Start by extracting the pulp from the mango. In a blender, combine the mango pulp, lime juice, and apple cider vinegar until smooth. Gradually drizzle in the EVOO while the blender is running. This will help in emulsifying the mixture. Once you achieve a smooth consistency, transfer the vinaigrette to a bowl. Stir in the finely chopped basil, salt, and black pepper. Adjust seasoning if necessary.

N.V.: 85 calories, 1g protein, 7g fat, 6g carbohydrates.

Recipe 2: Citrus Ginger Glow

P.T.: 8 minutes

Ingr.: Juice of 1 orange, juice of half a lemon, 1 teaspoon freshly grated ginger, 2 tablespoons sesame oil, 1 tablespoon soy sauce, 1 tablespoon honey or maple syrup, and a sprinkle of sesame seeds.

Serves: 4

M. of C.: Whisking

Process: In a bowl, whisk together the orange and lemon juices. Add in the freshly grated ginger, followed by the sesame oil, ensuring you whisk continuously for a homogenous mix. Stir in the soy sauce and sweetener of choice. Once combined, garnish with sesame seeds.

N.V.: 70 calories, 0.5g protein, 5g fat, 6g carbohydrates.

Recipe 3: Green Avocado Tango

P.T.: 10 minutes

Ingr.: Flesh of 1 ripe avocado, 2 tablespoons fresh cilantro chopped, juice of 1 lime, 2 tablespoons EVOO, 1 garlic clove minced, salt to taste, and a splash of water to adjust consistency.

Serves: 4-5

M. of C.: Blending

Process: Combine avocado flesh, cilantro, lime juice, and garlic in a blender. As the blend becomes smooth, slowly pour in the EVOO to maintain a creamy texture. Add water if you want a thinner consistency. Season with salt and blend again for a final mix.

N.V.: 110 calories, 1g protein, 10g fat, 5g carbohydrates.

Recipe 4: Pomegranate Pepper Punch

P.T.: 7 minutes

Ingr.: ½ cup fresh pomegranate juice, 1 tablespoon balsamic vinegar, 3 tablespoons EVOO, 1 teaspoon freshly cracked black pepper, and salt to taste.

Serves: 4

M. of C.: Mixing

Process: In a jug, mix the pomegranate juice and balsamic vinegar. Slowly stream in the EVOO while continuously stirring to get a cohesive mixture. Season with black pepper and salt.

N.V.: 90 calories, 0.2g protein, 8g fat, 4g carbohydrates.

Recipe 5: Raspberry Rosemary Delight

P.T.: 9 minutes

Ingr.: ½ cup fresh raspberries, 1 sprig fresh rosemary finely chopped, 2 tablespoons red wine vinegar, 3 tablespoons EVOO, 1 tablespoon honey, and a pinch of salt.

Serves: 4

M. of C.: Blending

Process: Add raspberries and red wine vinegar to a blender and process until smooth. Introduce the EVOO slowly to the mixture. Transfer to a bowl and fold in the chopped rosemary, honey, and salt.

N.V.: 80 calories, 0.3g protein, 7g fat, 5g carbohydrates.

Cook with Juice: Creative Culinary Use

Recipe 1: Orange-Infused Quinoa Salad

P.T.: 25 minutes

Ingr.: 1 cup quinoa, 2 cups water, juice of 2 oranges, zest of 1 orange, 1 cup diced bell peppers, ½ cup chopped fresh parsley, ¼ cup chopped dried apricots, salt and pepper to taste, 2 tablespoons EVOO.

Serves: 4

M. of C.: Boiling and Mixing

Process: Begin by rinsing the quinoa under cold water. In a saucepan, combine the quinoa, water, and half of the orange juice. Bring the mixture to a boil, reduce heat, cover, and let it simmer until quinoa is tender and the water has been absorbed. Once cooked, transfer to a bowl and let it cool. Add bell peppers, parsley, and apricots to the quinoa. For the dressing, whisk together the remaining orange juice, orange zest, EVOO, salt, and pepper. Pour this over the quinoa mix, stirring well to combine.

N.V.: 210 calories, 6g protein, 5g fat, 40g carbohydrates.

Recipe 2: Lemon Grass Chicken Stir Fry

P.T.: 30 minutes

Ingr.: 500g boneless chicken cubes, juice of 1 lemon, 2 stalks of lemongrass finely chopped, 2 tablespoons soy sauce, 1 tablespoon honey, 1 tablespoon EVOO, 1 cup sliced bell peppers, 2 minced garlic cloves.

Serves: 4

M. of C.: Sautéing

Process: Marinate the chicken cubes with lemon juice, lemongrass, soy sauce, and honey for at least 15 minutes. In a wok, heat the EVOO and sauté the garlic till fragrant. Add the chicken cubes, and cook until they're no longer pink. Toss in bell peppers and cook for another 5-7 minutes. Adjust seasoning if needed.

N.V.: 220 calories, 25g protein, 7g fat, 15g carbohydrates.

Recipe 3: Apple Cider Braised Red Cabbage

P.T.: 40 minutes

Ingr.: 1 medium-sized red cabbage finely sliced, ½ cup apple cider, 1 red onion thinly sliced, 2 tablespoons brown sugar, salt and pepper to taste, 2 tablespoons butter.

Serves: 4-5

M. of C.: Braising

Process: In a large pot, melt butter and sauté onions until translucent. Add in red cabbage, stirring occasionally until slightly wilted.

Sprinkle brown sugar, followed by apple cider. Allow the mixture to come to a boil, then reduce heat, cover, and simmer. Cook until cabbage is tender and has absorbed most of the liquid. Season with salt and pepper.

N.V.: 110 calories, 2g protein, 5g fat, 15g carbohydrates.

Recipe 4: Tomato Basil Pasta with Pineapple Reduction

P.T.: 35 minutes

Ingr.: 200g spaghetti, 1 cup tomato basil sauce, juice of 1 ripe pineapple, 1 teaspoon red chili flakes, salt to taste, 2 tablespoons EVOO, parmesan cheese for garnishing.

Serves: 3-4

M. of C.: Boiling and Sautéing

Process: Boil the spaghetti until al dente. In a separate pan, pour in pineapple juice and bring it to a boil. Reduce the heat and let it simmer until the juice reduces to half its quantity, creating a thick sauce. In a skillet, heat EVOO and add chili flakes. Pour tomato basil sauce and stir. Introduce the pineapple reduction and let it simmer for a couple of minutes. Toss in the boiled spaghetti, ensuring it's coated with the sauce. Garnish with parmesan cheese.

N.V.: 290 calories, 8g protein, 8g fat, 50g carbohydrates.

Recipe 5: Grape Juice Glazed Carrots

P.T.: 20 minutes

Ingr.: 500g baby carrots, ½ cup red grape juice, 2 tablespoons honey, salt to taste, 2 tablespoons butter, chopped parsley for garnishing.

Serves: 4

M. of C.: Glazing

Process: In a pan, melt butter and add carrots. Sauté them for a few minutes. Pour in grape juice and honey, stirring occasionally. Allow the juice to reduce until it forms a glaze on the carrots. Ensure carrots are tender and fully coated with the glaze. Season with salt and garnish with parsley.

N.V.: 130 calories, 1g protein, 6g fat, 20g carbohydrates.

The culinary world is boundless, and by incorporating juices into your dishes, you've expanded the horizon of possibilities in your kitchen. Whether you're dressing a salad or braising a vegetable, the juices add an element of surprise, nutrition, and depth. Here's to celebrating the union of nutrition and gastronomy, to creating dishes that are both delightful to the palate and nourishing for the body.

Chapter 12: Beyond Juices: Incorporating Smoothies

In the dance of health and nutrition, our steps often lead us beyond the simple allure of freshly squeezed juices. Enter the world of smoothies, where blending takes center stage, and whole ingredients whirl into rich symphonies of taste and texture. Just as a maestro appreciates every instrument in an orchestra, understanding the nuances between juicing and blending can elevate our nutritional journey. As we delve into this world, we'll unravel the distinctive nutritional perspectives of both methods and explore the art of crafting well-balanced smoothies, adding rhythm to our wellness routine.

Blend vs. Juice: A Nutritional Perspective

In the realm of beverages designed for optimal health, two titans stand head-to-head: blended smoothies and fresh juices. Each offers a myriad of nutritional benefits, each touts its own merits, and both have found passionate ambassadors in the world of health enthusiasts. Yet, when we drill down into the very essence of these two beverages, distinct differences emerge. It's not merely about texture or preparation; it's a holistic differentiation in nutritional content, absorption rates, and purpose.

Blending and juicing are two sides of the same coin, with each process illuminating unique facets of the ingredients used. The very act of blending churns whole fruits and vegetables into a viscous concoction, ensuring that the fibers, often referred to as the roughage of the plants, remain intact. Fiber, as we're well aware, is an unsung hero in the nutritional world. It aids digestion, helps maintain blood sugar levels, and keeps our gut flora balanced. It also offers a satiating quality, making you feel full and, in turn, aiding in weight management.

On the other hand, juicing extracts the liquid essence from fruits and vegetables, leaving behind the pulp and the fibers. But this isn't a shortcoming. Juices are like nature's very own elixir, a potent potion that can flood our systems with vitamins, minerals, and antioxidants in one fell swoop. Without the presence of fiber, our body can rapidly absorb these nutrients. For those seeking immediate nourishment, especially after a rigorous workout session or a taxing day, juices are akin to a veritable nutrient IV drip.

But as with everything in life, balance is key. While smoothies offer the advantage of fibers and can often double up as a meal replacement, they can also become calorie dense if one's not careful. Tossing in handfuls of nuts, scoops of protein powders, dollops of nut butter – all of these can quickly ramp up the calorie count. For someone monitoring their intake, the satiety offered by smoothies may come at the cost of higher calories.

Conversely, juices, devoid of fiber, can sometimes cause a spike in blood sugar levels, especially if they're primarily fruit-based. Without the moderating influence of fiber, the sugars in the juice can get rapidly absorbed. While this isn't a concern for everyone, individuals with conditions like diabetes might need to approach juicing with caution.

The blending process also retains another essential component: fat. Yes, in today's era, we've thankfully debunked the myth that fats are the villains of nutrition. Fats are vital. They assist in the absorption of fat-soluble vitamins like A, D, E, and K. A smoothie with avocado or chia seeds not only offers a creamy texture but also ensures that the body assimilates all the vitamins present efficiently.

On the flip side, the rapid absorption feature of juices can be ingeniously used for detox purposes. A pure, green vegetable juice, for instance, can offer a quick flush of nutrients, antioxidants, and enzymes that can help cleanse the system. The absence of fiber means the digestive system gets a brief respite, allowing the body to focus its energies on detoxification and repair.

The beauty of both these beverages lies in their adaptability. Based on one's needs – be it detoxification, meal replacement, post-workout nourishment, or merely a refreshing drink – one can opt for either a juice or a smoothie. But to pit them against each other would be a disservice to both.

The allure of smoothies and juices isn't merely about their health benefits. It's about the ritual of creation. Selecting fresh produce, washing them, prepping, and finally seeing them transform into a vibrant drink is therapeutic. It's an affirmation of one's commitment to nourishment and well-being.

To encapsulate, the debate between blend and juice isn't about superiority. It's about understanding. Knowing the unique benefits of each can empower individuals to make informed choices based on their specific needs and health goals. Both are delightful companions in the journey of wellness, offering their individual tales of nutrition and well-being. So the next time you're standing before your blender or juicer, take a moment to appreciate the magic they're about to create, and the myriad ways they're about to enrich your health.

Crafting Balanced Smoothies: A Recipe Guide

Recipe 1: Dragon's Embrace Smoothie

P.T.: 10 minutes

Ingr.: Half a dragon fruit (peeled and chopped), 1 cup frozen blueberries, 1 tablespoon chia seeds, 2 cups almond milk, 1 tablespoon agave nectar, and a pinch of pink Himalayan salt.

Serves: 2

M. of C.: Blending

Process: Begin by ensuring all ingredients are at hand. In a high-speed blender, combine the dragon fruit, blueberries, chia seeds, almond milk, and agave nectar. Blend on high until the mixture achieves a creamy consistency. Taste and adjust sweetness if necessary by adding more agave nectar. Add a pinch of pink Himalayan salt and give it a quick pulse. Pour into glasses and serve immediately.

N.V.: This smoothie contains 180 kcal, 4g of protein, 5g of fat, and 32g of carbohydrates.

Recipe 2: Tropical Greens Fusion

P.T.: 10 minutes

Ingr.: 1 cup fresh spinach, 1/2 avocado, 1 cup pineapple chunks, 1 tablespoon flax seeds, 2 cups coconut water, and 1 teaspoon spirulina powder.

Serves: 2

M. of C.: Blending

Process: Combine spinach, avocado, pineapple, flax seeds, and coconut water in a blender. Blend until smooth. Introduce spirulina powder and blend again until fully integrated. Serve in tall glasses.

N.V.: The fusion contains 210 kcal, 4g of protein, 9g of fat, and 30g of carbohydrates.

Recipe 3: Berry Bliss Booster

P.T.: 10 minutes

Ingr.: 1 cup mixed berries (strawberries, blueberries, raspberries), 1/2 cup Greek yogurt, 2 cups oat milk, 2 tablespoons honey, and 1 tablespoon hemp seeds.

Serves: 2

M. of C.: Blending

Process: In a blender, combine mixed berries, Greek yogurt, oat milk, and honey. Blend until creamy and smooth. Sprinkle hemp seeds and blend for another 20 seconds. Pour and serve chilled.

N.V.: This booster provides 230 kcal, 7g of protein, 5g of fat, and 42g of carbohydrates.

Recipe 4: Choco-Nut Energizer

P.T.: 10 minutes

Ingr.: 2 ripe bananas, 1 tablespoon cocoa powder, 2 tablespoons peanut butter, 2 cups soy milk, and 1 tablespoon maple syrup.

Serves: 2

M. of C.: Blending

Process: Peel and break the bananas into smaller chunks. Place them in a blender with cocoa powder, peanut butter, soy milk, and maple syrup. Blend until you attain a velvety consistency. Serve immediately with a sprinkle of cocoa on top.

N.V.: The energizer contains 280 kcal, 9g of protein, 10g of fat, and 40g of carbohydrates.

Recipe 5: Cinnamon Oat Delight

P.T.: 12 minutes

Ingr.: 1/2 cup rolled oats, 1 apple (peeled and chopped), 1 teaspoon cinnamon powder, 2 cups almond milk, 2 tablespoons honey, and 1 tablespoon sunflower seeds.

Serves: 2

M. of C.: Blending

Process: Soak rolled oats in almond milk for about 10 minutes. In a blender, combine the soaked oats, apple, cinnamon powder, and honey. Blend until creamy. Garnish with sunflower seeds and serve.

N.V.: The delight has 220 kcal, 6g of protein, 6g of fat, and 38g of carbohydrates.

With every sip of a meticulously blended smoothie or a carefully pressed juice, we imbibe more than just nutrients; we savor the stories and intentions behind each preparation. By embracing the unique benefits of both blending and juicing, we open doors to diversified paths of wellness. As we continue our dance, may we always celebrate the symphony of flavors, textures, and health benefits that both smoothies and juices bring into our lives.

Chapter 13: Meal plain 30 days

Embarking on a thirty-day culinary journey is like immersing oneself in a vibrant dance of flavors, each step leading seamlessly to the next, promising not just nourishment but also a sensory delight. With a plethora of recipes at hand, spanning from citrus wonders to rich, nutty concoctions, this meal plan is meticulously crafted to ensure every day brings a fresh gustatory experience. Diverse in ingredients and packed with health benefits, every meal is designed to be both a treat to the palate and a step toward holistic well-being.

Days 1-10

Day	Breakfast	Lunch	Dinner	Snack
1	Citrus Sunrise Elixir	Orange-Infused Quinoa Salad	Lemon Grass Chicken Stir Fry	Walnut Waltz Elixir
2	Lime Luster Splash	Tomato Basil Pasta with Pineapple Reduction	Apple Cider Braised Red Cabbage	Pecan Praline Pleasure
3	Tangerine Tango Twist	Crimson Drizzle	Grape Juice Glazed Carrots	Coconut Charm Whisper
4	Golden Citrus Medley	Ruby Radiance	Cucumber Cascade	Hazel Harmony Brew
5	Ruby Grapefruit Glory	Indigo Infusion	Watermelon Wave	Pistachio Poise Potion
6	Verdant Vitality Boost	Scarlet Serenity	Pineapple Pacific	Amber Ambrosia
7	Spinach Soothe	Golden Glimmer	Coconut Bliss Burst	Emerald Euphoria
8	Broccoli Brilliance	Lavender Luminescence	Ginger Green Quench	Sienna Serendipity
9	Zucchini Zen	Verdant Vitalizer	Golden Elixir Surge	Peridot Pleasure
10	Cabbage Calm	Turmeric Tonic	Spirulina Powerhouse	Jade Jubilation

Days 11-20

Day	Breakfast	Lunch	Dinner	Snack
11	Peachy Purity	Minty Beet Bliss	Beetroot Vitality Vial	Basil Bliss Boost
12	Melon Mélange	Gingered Green Glory	Pineapple Paradigm Punch	Minty Melon Elixir
13	Berry Bliss	Cilantro Citrus Cleaner	Moringa Morning Motivator	Thyme Thrive Tonic
14	Pearlescent Pleasure	Cucumber Cascade	Dragon's Embrace Smoothie	Rosemary Radiance Refresher
15	Mangosteen Marvel	Durian Delight	Tropical Greens Fusion	Lavender Love Liqueur
16	Rambutan Reverie	Jackfruit Jubilation	Berry Bliss Booster	Clove & Cranberry Cooler
17	Carambola Concoction	Citrus Ginger Glow	Choco-Nut Energizer	Cinnamon Sunrise
18	Verdant Vitalizer	Green Avocado Tango	Cinnamon Oat Delight	Peppered Pineapple
19	Turmeric Tonic	Pomegranate Pepper Punch	Avocado Almond Symphony	Cardamom Citrus Fusion
20	Minty Beet Bliss	Raspberry Rosemary Delight	Berry Oat Odyssey	Star Anise Apple Aid

Days 21-30

Day	Breakfast	Lunch	Dinner	Snack
21	Gingered Green Glory	Mango Basil Vinaigrette	Nut Butter Bliss	Cocoa Coconut Creaminess
22	Cilantro Citrus Cleaner	Golden Elixir Surge	Green Grain Galore	Mango Mousse Magic
23	Cucumber Cascade	Spirulina Powerhouse	Choco-Chia Dream	Berrylicious Pudding Punch
24	Watermelon Wave	Beetroot Vitality Vial	Creamy Kiwi Concoction	Caramel Apple Euphoria
25	Pineapple Pacific	Moringa Morning Motivator	Berry Oat Odyssey	Avocado Almond Symphony
26	Coconut Bliss Burst	Dragon's Embrace Smoothie	Nut Butter Bliss	Cocoa Coconut Creaminess
27	Ginger Green Quench	Tropical Greens Fusion	Green Grain Galore	Mango Mousse Magic
28	Golden Elixir Surge	Berry Bliss Booster	Choco-Chia Dream	Berrylicious Pudding Punch
29	Spirulina Powerhouse	Choco-Nut Energizer	Creamy Kiwi Concoction	Caramel Apple Euphoria
30	Beetroot Vitality Vial	Cinnamon Oat Delight	Avocado Almond Symphony	Cocoa Coconut Creaminess

As we wrap up our month-long culinary voyage, we come to appreciate not just the diversity of flavors that nature offers, but also the infinite ways they can be combined to create delightful meals. While each day presented a unique combination, the underlying thread was a commitment to health and taste. Let this not be an endpoint, but rather a springboard. May the past thirty days inspire countless more filled with delicious exploration and joyous eating.

Part V: Appendices

Appendix A: Nutritional Value and Calorie Count of Popular Ingredients

Stepping into the world of health, nutrition, and wellness often feels like embarking on an expedition. Just like a seasoned traveler knows the landmarks, routes, and histories of the places they visit, our wellness journey requires us to understand the terrains and treasures of our dietary landscape. One such indispensable map in this endeavor is the chart of nutritional values and calorie counts of the foods we consume.

When you think of nutrition, what comes to mind? Maybe you see a kaleidoscope of vibrant vegetables and fruits. Perhaps you think of proteins in lean meats or the warmth of wholesome grains. Whatever your mind's eye conjures, the universal truth remains: each food item is a tapestry of nutritional elements. To truly understand the impact of our diet, we must dive deeper into the wellspring of nutrition each ingredient offers.

Let's embark on this voyage by examining an apple, often dubbed the quintessential fruit. Hailing from the orchards, this crimson and golden delight isn't just a treat for the taste buds but is a treasure trove of nutrients. A medium-sized apple, with its skin, is a modest 95 calories. It isn't just the calories that make it notable. With its dietary fiber, it aids digestion and offers vitamin C, which bolsters immunity. It's not about counting the calories but counting on the right calories.

Similarly, take almonds, a favorite among snack enthusiasts and health aficionados alike. A handful, approximately 23 almonds, provides 164 calories. But don't let the calorie count overshadow the vast nutrition these nuts pack. Almonds brim with healthy fats, magnesium, and vitamin E, essentials that support heart health, bone health, and even your skin's radiance. It's a wonder how such a small nut can hold an abundance of nutrients!

As we voyage further, let's drop our anchor at the shores of the spinach territory. Often spotlighted in salads and smoothies, this leafy green is a mere 7 calories per cup when raw. Yet, its calorie count barely scratches the surface of its nutritional might. A powerhouse of iron, calcium, and vitamins A, C, and K, spinach is a testament to the fact that, sometimes, the best things truly come in small, leafy packages.

In contrast, when we explore the realm of grains, rice emerges as a staple for many cultures. A cup of cooked white rice is about 204 calories. While it might seem plain, rice is a source of energy, providing essential carbohydrates. It also offers proteins and traces of vitamins, making it a canvas for various cuisines and dishes worldwide.

While these illustrations paint a vivid image, it's essential to remember that the calorie count doesn't always narrate the full story of any food. For instance, avocados are relatively high in calories compared to other fruits. However, their monounsaturated fat content, which is heart-friendly, and their abundance of vitamins and minerals, make them a nutritional gem.

In the grand theatre of nutrition, it's not just about the leading actors but also about the supporting cast. Elements like fiber in beans, antioxidants in berries, or the probiotics in yogurt play roles just as crucial as primary nutrients. Each ingredient, irrespective of its calorie count, holds its unique place in the symphony of nutrition.

In our pursuit of health, understanding the nutritional value and calorie count is akin to having a compass. It doesn't dictate our path but guides us, ensuring we're nourished and satiated. Whether you're designing a meal, picking a snack, or indulging in a treat, having a grasp on the nutritional background can be the difference between merely eating and truly nourishing oneself.

By embracing the stories and nuances behind each calorie and nutrient, we're not just feeding our bodies; we're fueling our souls, ensuring that every bite taken is a step toward holistic wellness.

Appendix B: Seasonality and Storage Charts for Fruits and Vegetables

Produce	Seasonality	Storage
Watermelon	Summer	Cool, dry place; refrigerate once cut
Pumpkin	Autumn	Cool, dry place; refrigerate once cut or cooked

Produce	Seasonality	Storage
Strawberries	Spring - Early Summer	Refrigerate in breathable containers; wash before use
Potatoes	All year	Cool, dark place (away from onions)
Carrots	All year	Refrigerate in plastic bags; remove greens
Onions	All year	Cool, dark, dry place in mesh bag or basket
Spinach	Spring/Fall	Refrigerate wrapped in paper towels
Arugula	Spring/Fall	Refrigerate wrapped in paper towels
Apples	Fall	Countertop or refrigerator; away from other produce
Bananas	All year	Room temperature; refrigerator to slow ripening
Blueberries	Summer	Refrigerate; wash before use
Broccoli	Fall/Spring	Refrigerate in plastic bags; use within a week
Peaches	Summer	Room temperature until ripe, then refrigerate
Tomatoes	Summer	Room temperature; avoid refrigeration
Peppers	Summer - Fall	Refrigerate in plastic bags
Cucumbers	Summer	Refrigerate in plastic bags
Kale	All year, best in cold months	Refrigerate wrapped in paper towels
Oranges	Winter	Room temperature or refrigerator
Pears	Late Summer - Early Winter	Room temperature until ripe, then refrigerate
Grapes	Late Summer - Fall	Refrigerate; wash before use

BONUS

Challenges, Solutions, and Keeping Motivated

Diving into the realm of juicing can feel much like venturing into a dense, uncharted jungle. The allure of radiant health, increased energy, and a renewed zest for life beckons. Yet, hidden behind the lush foliage lie inevitable challenges, capable of stalling even the most ardent of enthusiasts. The path forward? It's one of resilience, creativity, and unyielding motivation.

Let's begin with the challenges. Picture this: After a week of diligently juicing, savoring the vibrant flavors, and reveling in newfound energy, the first hiccup surfaces. Perhaps it's the monotony of daily preparation, or maybe it's the daunting price of organic produce. Such practical issues are just the tip of the proverbial iceberg. Soon, the temptation of processed foods or the occasional jeer from a skeptical friend might add to the mounting challenges.

But here's the beautiful part. Every challenge, no matter its form, holds within it the seed of a solution waiting to germinate. Let's address the aforementioned. Feeling the monotony? One could rekindle excitement by exploring an exotic fruit or an unfamiliar vegetable. The high price of organic produce can be circumvented by local farmer markets or even growing one's herbs. As for naysayers, remember, every individual's health journey is intensely personal. It's essential to appreciate and respect the unique rhythm of one's path.

However, the physical or logistical challenges are often easier to navigate compared to the emotional and psychological ones. The human spirit, though resilient, can occasionally buckle under the weight of self-doubt, impatience, or sheer exhaustion. The solution here isn't external; it's a deep, introspective journey. Reflect upon the 'why' behind your juicing endeavor. Is it the allure of radiant health? The desire to break free from the clutches of processed foods? Or is it a quest to discover the authentic, vibrant version of oneself? When the 'why' is clear, the 'how' becomes an exciting adventure rather than a tedious chore.

Drawing upon the wisdom of countless individuals who've walked this path, a universal truth emerges: The journey of juicing, like any worthwhile endeavor, isn't a linear one. It's paved with peaks of exhilaration and valleys of despair. Yet, with every valley traversed, one emerges stronger, wiser, and more committed.

Let's consider Sarah, a dedicated juicer. Her initial days were euphoric, but the charm soon waned as the routine set in. But instead of surrendering, Sarah leaned into the challenge. She formed a community, a small group of like-minded enthusiasts. They would share recipes, swap ingredients, and often juice together. This not only rekindled her passion but also fortified her commitment. The lesson here is clear: community and shared experiences can be a powerful antidote to waning motivation.

The act of juicing, beyond its evident nutritional merits, is a celebration of the human spirit's ability to evolve, adapt, and thrive. Challenges will arise, as they always do. But with a clear vision, a heart brimming with passion, and a community to lean on, these challenges transform into stepping stones, propelling one towards their highest potential.

So, as you pour that next glass of juice, let it be a toast. A toast to the journey, the challenges, the solutions, and the indomitable spirit that keeps us moving forward, one sip at a time.

Navigating Through Challenges

The vibrant world of juicing is much akin to sailing on vast, unending waters. There's the thrill of discovery, the joy of basking in nature's bounty, and the myriad colors and flavors that enthrall our senses. But as every seasoned sailor knows, calm seas don't make a skilled sailor. It's the unpredictable waves, the sudden storms, and the rogue winds that truly test and hone one's skills. In the same breath, the path of juicing, despite its allure, is not without its fair share of challenges.

Imagine setting sail with a clear blue sky, only to find dark clouds looming ahead. In the world of juicing, this could equate to that first encounter with a juice blend that doesn't quite hit the mark in taste. Or perhaps it's that realization that cleaning the juicer isn't as breezy as one had imagined. Maybe it's the subtle realization that the initial days of excitement have now morphed into a routine, and the spark seems to be waning.

So, how does one navigate through these challenges? The first step is in acknowledging them, not as deterrents, but as integral facets of the journey. Every challenge met is a lesson learned, a skill honed, a perspective broadened.

Consider the challenge of stumbling upon a less-than-palatable juice blend. Instead of discarding the experience, dive into the world of flavors. Understand the intricate dance of sweet, sour, bitter, and tangy. Maybe that kale needed the sweetness of a pineapple or the zest of a lemon. It's a delightful alchemy, one where the journey is as enriching as the destination.

Cleaning and maintenance of the juicer, on the other hand, are undeniably tedious. But here's a fresh perspective. Think of it as a ritual, a grounding practice where one cares for the tools that catalyze the transformation of raw ingredients into liquid gold. Over time, this 'chore' can become a meditative practice, an exercise in mindfulness and gratitude.

And then there's the elephant in the room—the waning spark, the fading novelty. Here, the trick is to continuously reinvent and rediscover. Set monthly themes: tropical blends, detox specials, or even color-themed weeks. Dive into the stories and histories of exotic fruits and vegetables. Did you know that the vibrant dragon fruit is also called the "moonflower" because it blooms at night? Such nuggets of wisdom add layers of depth to the experience.

One might also find inspiration in others' journeys. Join a community or a group dedicated to juicing. Share stories, trade recipes, and celebrate milestones. Such camaraderie can be the wind beneath the wings, propelling one to stay the course even when the going gets tough.

Finally, in navigating challenges, embrace them as signposts that add depth and character to the story. Remember, the richest tales, the most memorable adventures, are never about the destinations alone; they are about the storms braved, the challenges met, and the resilience displayed. In the world of juicing, it's not just about the glass filled with vibrant hues; it's about the journey of turning obstacles into stepping stones, making every sip a testament to the human spirit's unwavering resolve.

Addressing Common Hurdles

Just beyond the horizon of our juicing adventures lie those sneaky obstacles, the hurdles that have a habit of appearing when we least expect them. Yet, much like a seasoned traveler knows the intricacies of the terrains they tread, an avid juicer must recognize and adeptly navigate the common hurdles that might surface.

One such hurdle, rather ironically, springs from our love for diversity. With a plethora of fruits and vegetables available, sometimes the sheer magnitude of choices can be overwhelming. Do we opt for the kale or the spinach? The beets or the carrots? Sometimes, in the maze of colors, textures, and flavors, one can feel lost. The key is simplicity. Start with what you know, what you love. Build from there. The art of juicing isn't about crafting the most complex blend every time; it's about savoring the simplicity and the symphony of flavors even in the most basic combinations. Find solace in the familiar and then, with each passing day, inch towards the unfamiliar, one fruit, one vegetable at a time.

Another hurdle often encountered is the stark realization of the investment. High-quality juicers, organic produce, and other accouterments come with their price tags. The thought might sometimes flit across the mind: "Is this sustainable?" Here, perspective is paramount. Think of this as an investment in health, vitality, and well-being. Also, recognize that while the initial outlay might seem substantial, the long-term benefits, both tangible and intangible, far outstrip the costs. Yet, for the budget-conscious, strategies such as buying in bulk, choosing local produce, or even growing some basics in one's backyard can be effective.

Perhaps the most subtle and yet potent of hurdles is the internal dialogue. The voice that sometimes whispers, "Skip today, it's just one day." Or the voice that laments, "This is too hard." This is where the heart of resilience beats. Addressing this requires a blend of self-compassion and discipline. Understand that the journey is unique for each individual. There will be days of unbridled enthusiasm and days of contemplative silence. On those challenging days, remind oneself of the 'why'. Why did the journey start? Was it health? Vitality? Curiosity? That 'why' is the beacon that can guide through the foggiest of days.

Another hurdle is the evolving palate. Initially, a juice might taste divine. But after having it repeatedly, the taste buds yearn for something new. This is a delightful hurdle, for it invites creativity. Dive deep into the ocean of flavors. Mix and match. Create and recreate. This hurdle isn't a roadblock; it's an invitation.

And then, there are external voices. Friends or family who might not understand the passion for juicing. Their skepticism, often born out of concern, can sometimes feel like a weight. Here, communication is the bridge. Share the joy, the vitality, and the newfound energy. Make them a part of the journey, even if just as spectators. Over time, the shared stories, the visible benefits, and the sheer joy of the process might just make them advocates.

In addressing these hurdles, remember that every challenge is an opportunity in disguise. An opportunity to learn, to grow, to evolve. The world of juicing, with its vibrant hues and myriad flavors, is also a world of patience, resilience, and unending discovery. Embrace the hurdles, for they are the stepping stones to a richer, deeper, more flavorful adventure.

FAQs and Quick Solutions

The rhythm of our world today is more of a fervent dance than a slow waltz, so it's no surprise that when a question emerges, we yearn for an answer that's both swift and satisfying. In the realm of juicing, with its intricate tapestries of flavors and nuances, certain questions repeatedly make their presence felt. So, let's dive deep into this treasure trove of inquiries and provide solutions that sparkle with clarity.

Question: Why does my juice taste different even when I use the same ingredients every time?

Ah, the ever-changing symphony of nature! Fruits and vegetables, despite their category labels, aren't factory-produced goods. They evolve with seasons, weather conditions, and the soil they are nurtured in. This constant evolution means a slight variance in taste, texture, and even nutritional profile. Embrace this diversity; it's nature whispering tales of different terrains and climates into your ears.

Question: I've heard that juicing takes away all the fiber. Is that accurate?

It's a commonly held belief, but let's refine it. Juicing extracts the liquid essence from fruits and vegetables, which means a reduction in insoluble fiber. However, the soluble fiber, a significant component, often remains in the juice. If you're seeking to retain more fiber, consider blending or adding some of the pulp back into your juice.

Question: Can I store my juice for later?

Time is a fickle friend, especially to freshly squeezed juice. As soon as you juice, oxidation starts, leading to nutrient degradation. Ideally, drink it fresh. However, if you must, store it in an airtight container in the fridge for no more than 24 hours. Remember, with each passing moment, the vibrant life force diminishes a tad.

Question: My juice sometimes comes out too watery or too thick. Why is this so?

Consistency in juicing can be an elusive mistress, especially when you're navigating through different produce types. Watery output often stems from juicy fruits or veggies like watermelon or cucumber. On the flip side, ingredients such as bananas or avocados give a creamier texture. Finding your preferred consistency is a game of balance. Adjust the proportion of juicy to creamy ingredients to strike that perfect harmony.

Question: I've started juicing, but I'm feeling more tired. Isn't it supposed to energize me?

Ah, the paradox of healing! Often, when you embark on a healthier path, the body begins detoxifying. This release of toxins, while ultimately beneficial, can initially lead to fatigue, headaches, or mood swings. Listen to your body. If it persists, consider consulting a nutritionist to tailor your juice recipes to your specific needs.

Question: Why is my green juice turning brown?

Oxidation and enzyme reactions are the culprits here. Certain ingredients, especially leafy greens, oxidize quickly. To counter this, consume your green juice promptly. If storing is necessary, minimize oxidation by filling your storage container to the brim to reduce air exposure.

Question: Can I replace all my meals with juices?

While the allure of a juice cleanse is undeniable, remember that long-term sustenance solely on juices might deprive you of essential nutrients and proteins. Juices are a supplement, a vibrant addition to your dietary mosaic, not a replacement for whole meals.

As we journey through the vast terrains of juicing, questions will naturally arise. They are but signposts indicating our eagerness to learn, to delve deeper. While these answers address the common queries, remember that the realm of juicing is vast and ever-evolving. Keep the spirit of curiosity alive, for with each question, you're one step closer to mastering this exquisite art.

Maintaining Motivation and Consistency

The sun rose brilliantly today, casting its golden hue upon the world, symbolizing a fresh start, a new day. Much like this dawn, every journey we embark on commences with a burst of motivation and determination. The world of juicing is no exception. Beginning with a resolve, a vision of health, and vitality, we dive deep into this wholesome endeavor. But as with any journey, once the initial brilliance wanes, what keeps us pushing forward?

Maintaining motivation and ensuring consistency isn't always about the roaring fires of inspiration. More often, it's about the soft, glowing embers that provide warmth over an extended period. It's about creating an environment, both physically and mentally, that nurtures this persistent flame.

Imagine for a moment a garden, lush and verdant. This garden symbolizes our motivation. If left untended, it might still grow, but weeds will overrun it, and the plants might not flourish as they should. Similarly, our motivation needs regular nurturing, pruning, and care.

Firstly, understand the 'why' behind your journey. While the health benefits of juicing are undeniable, the reason one person starts might differ from another. Some seek a sanctuary from the chaos of unhealthy habits, while others might be on a quest for that sublime state of health. Dive deep within and unearth your personal reason. It's this 'why' that will act as a beacon, especially during times when the path seems clouded.

Next, establish a routine, but with a twist. Humans are creatures of habit, and once something becomes a part of our daily rhythm, it's easier to adhere to. However, the monotony of routine can be a double-edged sword, leading to boredom. The solution? Introduce elements of novelty. Experiment with flavors, rotate your ingredients seasonally, or even change the time of day you juice. This slight shift keeps the process fresh and invigorating.

Surround yourself with reminders of your journey's benefits. These can be tangible or intangible. Perhaps it's the feeling of lightness after consuming a freshly prepared juice or the radiant glow of your skin. On tougher days, these reminders act as gentle nudges, pushing you back on track.

Celebrate milestones, no matter how small. Did you successfully incorporate a new vegetable into your juice that you previously loathed? Or did you manage to juice consistently for a week? These victories, though they might seem minuscule, are stepping stones. By recognizing and celebrating them, you're not just rewarding yourself, but also reinforcing your commitment.

Connect with fellow juicing enthusiasts. There's a certain energy in shared passions, a force that propels us forward. Engage in conversations, share your unique recipes, or discuss challenges. This communion not only keeps the flame of motivation alive but also introduces different perspectives, further enriching your journey.

Lastly, remember to be kind to yourself. The path to consistency isn't a straight line; it's more akin to the ebbs and flows of a river. There might be days when you falter, but instead of berating yourself, recognize it as a part of the journey. With every stumble, there's a lesson, a deeper understanding of oneself.

In essence, maintaining motivation and ensuring consistency in the world of juicing is a dance. It's a dance between understanding one's deeper motivations, embracing routine yet introducing elements of novelty, celebrating milestones, and sharing the journey with like-minded souls. And like any dance, there will be moments of sheer exhilaration and moments of fatigue, but with the right tune, the dance continues, graceful and full of life.

Success Stories and Testimonials

Amid the canvas of life, stories paint vivid pictures that inspire, uplift, and transform. Stories breathe life into abstract concepts, tethering them to the real world and making them palpable. In the realm of juicing, tales of transformation echo with vibrancy, showcasing how simple fruits and vegetables, when embraced with intent, have the potential to rewrite one's health narrative.

Take Clara, a 30-year-old graphic designer. She found herself wading through a quagmire of fatigue, mental fog, and low energy. Every morning felt like an insurmountable challenge, every task a Herculean effort. The cascade of coffee cups on her desk were testimony to her constant battle against weariness. But it wasn't until a serendipitous encounter at a bookstore that Clara's world began to shift. Nestled amid bestsellers, a book on juicing caught her eye. A month into her new juicing regimen, Clara felt like she was reborn. Her mornings became buoyant, her thoughts clearer than a pristine lake. "It's as if," she often remarked, "I've been gifted a new reservoir of energy."

Juxtapose Clara's story with Raj's, a 45-year-old accountant. For Raj, numbers were a passion, but the scales, a constant adversary. The digits he saw every morning left him disheartened. Determined to shift the scales, both metaphorically and literally, Raj embarked on a juicing journey. Over months, not only did he shed the extra pounds, but he also discovered a zest for life previously unknown. His testimonial, filled with gratitude, reads, "Juicing didn't just change my weight; it transformed my perspective on life."

But it's not just the Claras and the Rajs of the world who've experienced transformation. Liam, a young father, shares a poignant tale. Watching his daughter frolic and play, he felt an overwhelming desire to provide her with the best. Yet, he was acutely aware of the gap between his aspirations and reality. Sedentary habits and unhealthy eating patterns had taken their toll. It was during a casual conversation with a friend that Liam stumbled upon the magic of juicing. As weeks turned into months, Liam felt his vitality returning. He wasn't just an observer anymore;

he became an active participant in his daughter's world. His words shimmer with emotion: "Each juice wasn't just a drink. It was a promise, a commitment to my daughter and myself."

Diverse as these stories are, a common thread weaves them together - the profound impact of juicing. It's not just about nutrients or health; it's about reclaiming life, rediscovering vitality, and rekindling passion.

Stories resonate because they're real. They aren't sugar-coated tales of overnight transformation but journeys, filled with ups and downs. It's in these oscillations that the essence of life lies. For every Clara, Raj, or Liam who found success, there were moments of doubt, of wanting to revert to old ways. But they persisted, fueled by belief and determination.

To those standing at the cusp of their juicing journey, these testimonials are not just stories. They are torchbearers, illuminating the path, showcasing that change, while challenging, is achievable. They remind us that while the journey is personal, the echoes of transformation are universal. In these tales of triumph, in these heartfelt testimonials, lies an invitation - to embrace the world of juicing, to let it weave its magic, and to pen a success story that's uniquely yours.

Your Juicing Journal and Reflective Practices

In the realm of self-transformation, the gentle art of reflection proves itself a most profound ally. When we embark on a journey, especially one as intimate as reshaping our health, the path is often interspersed with moments of elation, doubt, discovery, and learning. Recording these moments, these fragments of our evolution, becomes a testament to our journey, a tangible embodiment of our metamorphosis. Enter the Juicing Journal, a canvas where words merge with emotions, where experiences meld with introspection.

Visualize this: The sun is casting its first golden rays, you're sipping on your morning elixir of vibrant greens, and as the flavors dance on your palate, you pen down your thoughts. How did the juice make you feel? Was there a burst of invigoration? A momentary reminiscence of a forgotten memory, perhaps triggered by a particular taste? The Journal becomes a repository of these sensations, these fleeting moments that might otherwise drift into the abyss of oblivion.

Now, consider Emma. A fervent journaler, she recorded every nuance of her juicing journey. One day, she wrote about the newfound lightness she felt, both physically and mentally. Another day, her words cascaded onto the page, detailing her struggle to resist the seductive allure of a chocolate pastry. Through the crests and troughs, her Journal became a mirror, reflecting her vulnerabilities and strengths. On challenging days, revisiting her initial entries, brimming with hope and enthusiasm, became a beacon, guiding her back to her path.

Beyond the realm of juicing, this Journal transcends into a space of holistic reflection. Think about Samuel, who used his journaling time as an exercise in mindfulness. For him, it wasn't just about the juice. It was about the ambiance when he consumed it, the thoughts that flitted through his mind, the dreams from the previous night. His Juicing Journal metamorphosed into a diary of self-awareness.

Then, there's the dimension of creativity. As you delve deeper into the juicing world, you'll inevitably feel the urge to experiment. When a splash of pineapple juice elevates a mundane kale concoction into a tropical delight, wouldn't you want to remember that? Your Journal can chronicle these recipe evolutions, becoming both a historical record and a future guide.

But, how does one truly harness the potency of reflective practices in the context of juicing? It's not merely about jotting down what juice you consumed. Delve deeper. How did that particular combination make you feel? Were you satiated, or left wanting? Energetic or surprisingly sluggish? Over time, these reflections reveal patterns, offering insights into what your body resonates with.

Reflective practices, when intertwined with the act of journaling, become a conduit for self-dialogue. It's a space where you converse with yourself, where you question, introspect, and most importantly, listen. Such a practice, in the context of a journey as transformative as juicing, becomes indispensable.

To the uninitiated, a Juicing Journal might seem an ornamental accessory. But for those who've felt the undulating rhythms of a transformative journey, who've tasted the highs and endured the lows, the Journal morphs into a sanctuary. It stands as a testament to the journey, a reminder of the distance traveled, and the horizons yet to be explored.

Embrace this journey with your Journal as your confidante. Let it be the canvas where your experiences, reflections, and emotions converge. Let it be the chronicle of your unique odyssey in the entrancing world of juicing.

142a543d-8ea3-4568-a4e2-8a3b84c83092R01